D1571612

Blue Apron team: Jared Cluff, TJ DiFrancesco, Winnie Jeng, Lucas Kalina, Timothy F. Kemp, Claire King, James Molloy, Chris Montgomery, Ilia Papas, Judith Peña, Matt Salzberg, Christopher M. Sorensen, Matthew Wadiak and Rani Yadav.

Published by Blue Apron, Inc.
5 Crosby Street, 3rd Floor
New York, NY 10013
www.blueapron.com

Library of Congress Cataloguing-in-Publication Data

Winter Cooking with Blue Apron, A Collection of Simple, Seasonal Recipes: Vol. 1 / Blue Apron, Inc.—1st ed. p. cm.

ISBN 978-0-9905101-2-3

10 9 8 7 6 5 4 3 2 1

Printed in Canada by the Prolific Group

WINTER COOKING

WITH Blue Apron

A COLLECTION OF SIMPLE, SEASONAL RECIPES: *vol. 1*

Contents

Welcome to the Blue Apron kitchen.

At Blue Apron, our mission is to make incredible home cooking accessible to everyone—to the novice cook just getting started and to the experienced chef who considers the kitchen home.

We create simple, seasonally inspired recipes and send them to our customers every week, along with all the fresh ingredients—pre-measured and perfectly proportioned—to prepare a delicious and healthy dinner.

In this cookbook, we celebrate our mission, while welcoming in the season, with our favorite winter ingredients and meals.

Why Eat at Home

We started Blue Apron to tackle cooking on a nightly basis, not just on special occasions. Even the simplest homemade salad or creative sandwich contains more whole, unprocessed ingredients than nearly anything pre-made. That translates into serious flavor and high-quality nutrition, as well as the measureless satisfaction of having created a wonderful meal. Cooking at home is a habit. Our goal is to make recipes that will inspire our customers to make it a part of their daily lives.

Step by Step

The weekly recipe cards we send with our ingredients contain up to six steps, accompanied by easy-to-follow photos. We've translated this visual cooking style into this book, so if you're not sure what to do after reading the text, take a close look at the corresponding photo for the visual cue. It will show you exactly how brown your caramelized onions should be or what we mean by "slightly reduced in volume."

Winter Ingredients

Even as winter settles in and shakes out its dustings of snow, the fields are alive with produce. Piebald jewels of citrus brighten on the trees. At ground level, globes of budding cabbages are unfurling. And below the soil, beets and root vegetables are swelling with their sweet, earthy flavors.

It's a season of joy. Here, we've collected recipes that use our favorite winter produce. We've also taken the opportunity to celebrate two other groups of ingredients we find particularly suited to winter: nuts and spices. Their comforting warmth helps define the season and the cuisine that makes it truly special. Let's revel. Let's gather and use winter's unique bounty to create memories that go beyond the occasion and last all year long.

Lifelong Learning

The recipes in the first seven chapters of this book will help you master winter meals for two, but don't stop there! This volume also contains recipes for brand-new dishes and projects—including desserts and feasts designed to serve ten. Each of these debut recipes has received the full Blue Apron treatment: inspired ingredients, accessible directions and step-by-step photos. As always, all you'll need to make them are the ingredients listed, along with olive oil, salt, pepper and a passion for great food!

How to Use This Cookbook

At Blue Apron, seasonality is one of our most treasured principles. That's why we've organized this cookbook around groups of winter ingredients. From beets, to root vegetables, to potatoes, to cabbages, to spices, to nuts, to citrus—each chapter explores the depth and versatility of the season's warmest foods.

At the beginning of each chapter we've included a short essay that details the history of these groups, providing context and fun facts. We've also included a short series of Field Guides that identify specific varieties and provide short descriptions. Also, throughout the volume, look for our Supplier Stories. These are profiles of some of the farmers and vendors we work with to source the best food available.

We're inspired by their stories, and we're inspired by yours! That's why we've included an entire spread of pictures you've shared with us—of you, your friends and your families preparing delicious, nutritious meals at home.

We can't wait to cook these winter recipes with you!

—THE BLUE APRON TEAM

WITH ITS ABUNDANCE of root vegetables, hearty greens and warming spices, cooking in winter is an opportunity for celebration. As we spend more time indoors, the season strengthens our bonds with our families, friends and loved ones.

Winter cooking is full of life: crunchy nuts survive the snow; brightly-colored citrus fruits are ripening in the trees; the roots below ground are swelling with nutrients. In the inspired, simple recipes that follow, we stop to appreciate all that the end of the year has to offer.

Winter is also a time for reflection. Just as farmers plow back their fields and strategize for upcoming plantings, we think back on the year that has passed, and consider the year ahead of us.

At Blue Apron, we strive to follow the signals of the soil, and to cherish its diversity—an act that brings us closer to the Earth. We make plans for the coming year while enjoying the bounty that remains in this one.

We dedicate this book to you, to cooking together seasonally and to winter itself, for bringing us together in the kitchen.

—**TIMOTHY F. KEMP,**
CULINARY MANAGER

Citrus

FIELD GUIDE TO CITRUS

The following are some of our favorite heirloom and specialty varieties. The best place to find them is at your local farmers' market, or you can grow them yourself. The seeds are available through seed saver websites.

Bergamot: A hybrid of sweet lemons and bitter oranges. Grown in Italy since the 1400s. A popular ingredient in Earl Grey tea.

Blood Orange: Maroon-fleshed due to a special pigment that develops only at night when temperatures are cool. Dominant variety in Italy.

Buddha's Hand: A fragrant variety whose sections form individual skins. Unlike that of most citrus fruits, the pith is not bitter.

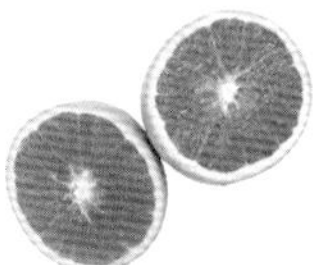

Cara Cara Orange: Discovered in Venezuela in 1976. A cross between the Washington navel and Brazilian Bahia navel.

Clementine: An accidental hybrid of mandarin and sweet oranges. First discovered in an Algerian orphanage by Friar Clement Rodier.

Eureka Lemon: The common lemon. Grown in California from Sicilian seeds as early as the 1850s. Main harvest is in late winter.

Finger Lime: An Australian variety recently brought back from near extinction. Long, tapered pods contain globes of juice called "lime caviar."

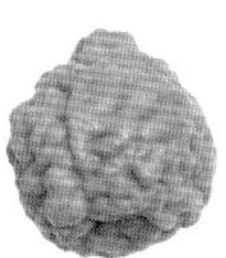

Makrut Lime: Also known as "kaffir lime." Native to Southeast Asia. Fruit and leaves are used in traditional cuisines, especially in Thailand.

Meyer Lemon: Native to China. A hybrid of sour and sweet citrus varieties. Introduced to the United States in 1908.

Navel Orange: A spontaneous variety traced back to Brazil. Grows a second fruit inside the same peel, leading to the "navel" opposite the stem.

Pink Variegated Lemon: A variation of the common lemon. Discovered in Burbank, CA, in the 1930s. Pink flesh and gorgeous, striped skin.

Pomelo: Pale, green and simply humongous. Has a sweet, mild flavor. Can be consumed raw and is used to make both desserts and liqueurs.

Ruby Red Grapefruit: The first grapefruit to be granted a U.S. patent. The red color comes from an accumulation of lycopene.

Satsuma Mandarin: Named for a province of Japan. Seedless and easily peeled. Jesuits brought the fruit from Asia to the Americas.

Seville Sour Orange: A cross between the pomelo and mandarin orange. Originally grown in Spain and shipped to England to make fine marmalades.

Tangelo: A juicy, sweet cross between grapefruit (or pomelo) and mandarin. Varieties include the Honeybell, Minneola and Orlando.

Tangerine: Native to Southeast Asia. Named for Tangiers, Morocco, from which it was first shipped to Europe and Florida in the 1800s.

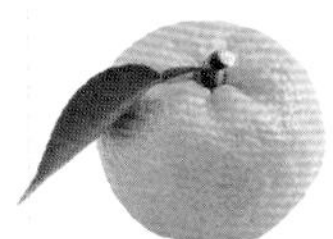

Yuzu: Bred in East Asia. First brought to America by the botanist Frank Meyer (of Meyer lemon fame).

CITRUS FRUITS HAVE stirred the taste buds and imaginations of human beings for millennia. Under their hard, colorful rinds and bitter, papery-white piths, these succulent fruits keep a secret. They're edible jewels: orange, pink, green, yellow, red. And from taste to texture, they're incomparably delicious.

Originally cultivated in China, citrus trees have gradually spread to the rest of the world. The first citrus fruit to be mentioned in Ancient Greek writing was the dry, zesty citron, which the father of botany, Theophrastus, called the "Median or Persian apple." Seventeen centuries later, European citrus cultivation had barely advanced: the sour orange had arrived, followed by the lemon, then the sweet orange in 1400 CE. The Chinese, meanwhile, had perfected some twenty-seven astonishing orange varieties, from

sour to sweet to mandarin. They'd even bred kumquats (miniature orange look-alikes with tender, edible rinds).

Though me may associate citrus with summer, wintertime is actually when they're at their best and brightest. After temperatures begin to cool, they store their juices and the essential oils concentrate in the rind.

Citrus is one of the most important ingredients in the kitchen and in most of our recipes. Chefs say they couldn't live without it. Citric acid, what makes citrus juice tart, is a culinary panacea. It brightens, adds contrast and connects flavors. If we were to imagine a meal as a brain, the individual flavors of the dish would be synapses, and lemon juice the electrical current that makes them fire, working together to create a fully-formed thought.

Fennel-Rubbed Pork Tenderloin

with Grapefruit, Mustard Greens & Japonica Black Rice

Grapefruit is a relative newcomer to the citrus family. It was discovered growing wild in the Caribbean in the 1700s (a natural variation on the sweet orange), and was originally called "forbidden fruit." Its current name comes from the grape-like clusters in which it grows. In this dish, you'll use it to cut the richness of pork and contrast the peppery zing of mustard greens. With an earthy, buttery side of black rice, this dish is a playful and striking balance of delightful flavors.

MAKES 2 SERVINGS • ABOUT 670 CALORIES PER SERVING

Ingredients

1 12-Ounce Pork Tenderloin
3-4 Sprigs Tarragon
2 Cloves Garlic
¾ Pound Mustard Greens
¾ Cup Japonica Black Rice
1 Grapefruit
2 Teaspoons Ground Fennel Seed
2 Tablespoons Butter

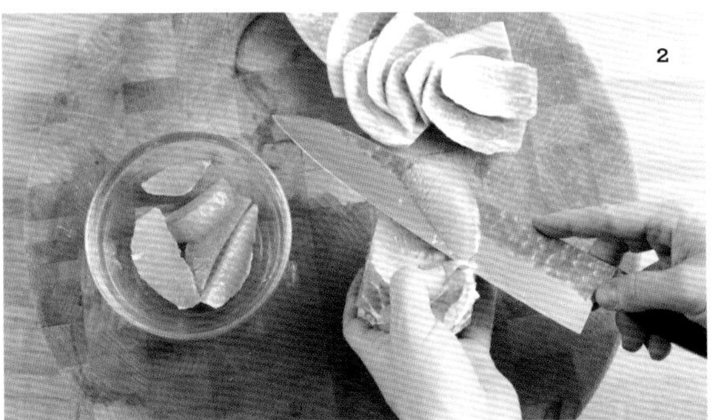

1 Prepare the ingredients

Preheat the oven to 500°F. Wash and dry the fresh produce. Heat a medium pot of salted water to boiling on high. Remove the pork tenderloin from the refrigerator to bring to room temperature. Pick the tarragon leaves off the stems; discard the stems and roughly chop the leaves. Peel and mince the garlic. Cut out and discard the thick stems of the mustard greens; roughly chop the leaves.

2 Cook the rice & prepare the grapefruit

Add the rice to the boiling water. Cook 15 to 20 minutes, or until tender. Drain thoroughly and return to the pot. While the rice cooks, using a knife, cut about ¼ inch off the top and bottom ends of the grapefruit and sit the grapefruit flat on a cutting board. Following the contour of the fruit, cut away and discard the peel and pith. Over a small bowl, cut out the individual segments (or supremes) from the thin membranes that separate them. Place the supremes in a small bowl. Squeeze the juice from the leftover membranes over the supremes.

3 Rub & roast the pork

While the rice cooks, pat the pork dry with paper towels and place on a sheet pan or baking dish. Season on all sides with salt, pepper and the ground fennel, then drizzle with a little olive oil. Using your hands, rub the seasonings into the pork. Place in the oven and roast, flipping halfway through, 18 to 20 minutes, or until cooked through (an instant-read thermometer should read 145°F). Remove from oven and let rest for at least 5 minutes before slicing.

4 Cook the mustard greens

In a large pan, melt half the butter with 2 teaspoons of olive oil on medium-high. Add the garlic; season with salt and pepper. Cook, stirring frequently, 30 seconds to 1 minute, or until softened and fragrant. Stir in the mustard greens; season with salt and pepper. Cook, stirring occasionally, 2 to 3 minutes, or until wilted. Season with salt and pepper to taste; remove from heat.

5 Finish & plate your dish

Stir the grapefruit juice (from the bowl of supremes) and the remaining butter into the cooked rice; season with salt and pepper. Toss the supremes with all but a pinch of the tarragon and 2 teaspoons of olive oil; season with salt and pepper to taste. Find the lines of muscle (or the grain) of the cooked pork. Slice the pork crosswise against the grain into ½-inch-thick pieces. Divide the pork between 2 dishes along with the dressed rice, mustard greens and grapefruit segments. Garnish with the remaining tarragon.

Blood Orange-Roasted Salmon

with Chickpea & Cucumber Salad

From the outside, a blood orange looks similar to a typical Valencia orange. But inside, its segmented pulp is a deep, beautiful maroon. The fruit gets its unique coloring from a special pigment that develops only at night, when temperatures are cool. (The pigment also supplies its almost berry-like flavor.) In this recipe, you'll place blood orange slices beneath and on top of the salmon before roasting to infuse the dish with their sweet, lightly tart flavor.

MAKES 2 SERVINGS • ABOUT 630 CALORIES PER SERVING

Ingredients

2 5-Ounce Skinless Salmon Fillets
2-3 Sprigs Dill
1 15.5-Ounce Can Chickpeas
1 Blood Orange
1 Clove Garlic
1 English Cucumber
1 Lemon
1 Small Red Onion
3-4 Sprigs Thyme
½ Cup Crumbled Goat Cheese

1 Prepare the ingredients

Preheat the oven to 450°F. Wash and dry the fresh produce. Remove the salmon from the refrigerator to bring to room temperature. Pick the dill off the stems; discard the stems and roughly chop the leaves. Drain and rinse the chickpeas. Without peeling, thinly slice the blood orange into rounds. Peel and mince the garlic; then, using the side of your knife, smash until it resembles a paste. Peel the cucumber and slice it in half lengthwise. Using a spoon, scoop out and discard the seeds; thinly slice the cucumber. Quarter the lemon and remove the seeds. Peel and thinly slice the onion.

2 Prepare the salmon

Pat the salmon fillets dry, then season with salt and pepper on both sides. Lightly oil a sheet pan and place half the blood orange slices and half the thyme sprigs in the middle of the pan. Place the seasoned salmon on top of the orange slices and thyme, pushing the 2 fillets together. Top with the remaining blood orange slices and remaining thyme sprigs. Drizzle with olive oil and season with salt and pepper.

3 Roast the salmon

Roast the salmon 15 to 20 minutes, or until cooked through. Remove from the oven. Carefully discard the thyme sprigs.

4 Make the salad

While the salmon roasts, in a large bowl, combine the cucumber, chickpeas, garlic paste, as much of the onion as you'd like (you may have extra onion), half the goat cheese and half the dill. Toss with the juice of all 4 lemon wedges and a drizzle of olive oil; season with salt and pepper to taste.

5 Finish & plate your dish

Divide the roasted salmon, blood orange slices and chickpea salad between 2 plates. Garnish with the remaining dill and remaining goat cheese.

White Chili

with Rainbow Chard & Tricolor Quinoa

Like most citrus fruit, the Meyer lemon was originally bred in China. A cross between a sour lemon and a sweet orange, Meyer lemons (named for an American explorer who traveled to Asia in search of new plants) are sweeter than typical Eureka or Lisbon lemons. In this dish, you'll mix their juice and zest with Greek yogurt to make a delicious, creamy sauce for tomato-less, white, sweet potato chili.

MAKES 2 SERVINGS • ABOUT 515 CALORIES PER SERVING

Ingredients

1 15-Ounce Can Cannellini Beans
5-6 Sprigs Cilantro
2 Cloves Garlic
1 Meyer Lemon
1 Poblano Pepper
1 Medium Sweet Potato
1 Yellow Onion
½ Pound Rainbow Swiss Chard
1¼ Teaspoons Ground Coriander
1¼ Teaspoons Ground Cumin
½ Teaspoon Smoked Paprika
¼ Cup Tricolor Quinoa
3 Tablespoons Vegetable Demi-Glace
¼ Cup Greek Yogurt

1 Prepare the ingredients

Wash and dry the fresh produce. Drain and rinse the cannellini beans. Pick the cilantro leaves off the stems; discard the stems. Peel and mince the garlic. Using a peeler, remove the yellow rind of the lemon, avoiding the white pith; mince the rind to get 2 teaspoons of zest. Quarter the lemon and remove the seeds. Remove the stem, seeds and ribs of the pepper; small dice the pepper. Peel and small dice the sweet potato and onion. Separate the chard leaves from the stems. Roughly chop the stems on an angle; chop the leaves into bite-sized pieces.

2 Cook the aromatics

In a large pot, heat 2 teaspoons of olive oil on medium-high until hot. Add the garlic and onion; season with salt and pepper. Cook, stirring frequently, 2 to 3 minutes, or until softened. Add the sweet potato, chard stems and all but a pinch of the poblano (save the rest for garnish); season with salt and pepper. Cook, stirring occasionally, 4 to 5 minutes, or until softened.

3 Toast the spices & quinoa

Add the coriander, cumin, paprika and quinoa to the pot. Cook, stirring frequently, 1 to 2 minutes, or until the spices and quinoa are toasted and fragrant.

4 Add the beans & demi-glace

Add the cannellini beans, vegetable demi-glace and 2 cups of water; season with salt and pepper. Bring to a boil. Once boiling, reduce the heat to medium-low and simmer, stirring occasionally, 8 to 10 minutes, or until slightly thickened and the quinoa is tender. Stir in the chard leaves; cook 2 to 3 minutes, or until wilted. Season with salt and pepper to taste.

5 Make the lemon yogurt & plate your dish

While the chili simmers, in a small bowl, combine the Greek yogurt, lemon zest, the juice of all 4 lemon wedges and 1 tablespoon water; season with salt and pepper to taste. To plate your dish, divide the chili between 2 dishes and top each with the lemon yogurt. Garnish with the cilantro and remaining poblano pepper.

Pan-Seared Cod

with Makrut Lime Butter Sauce

The makrut lime is a variety with bumpy skin native to South and Southeast Asia. It's most often used for its aromatic leaves. (You may be familiar with this ingredient from Thai or Lao dishes.) But don't neglect the fruit itself! In this dish, we're taking advantage of its fragrant astringency—and the exciting tang of its rind—to flavor couscous and a velvety butter sauce.

MAKES 2 SERVINGS • ABOUT 575 CALORIES PER SERVING

Ingredients

4 Baby Multicolored Carrots, Without Greens
4 Ounces Tatsoi
4 Sprigs Mint
3 Tablespoons Butter
1 Makrut Lime
1 Shallot
½ Cup Israeli Couscous
2 6-Ounce Cod Fillets
¼ Cup All-Purpose Flour

1 Prepare the ingredients

Preheat the oven to 500°F. Wash and dry the fresh produce. Heat a medium pot of salted water to boiling on high. Peel the carrots; halve the carrots lengthwise then cut at alternating angles into ½-inch pieces. Halve the tatsoi. Pick the mint leaves off the stems; discard the stems and roughly chop the leaves. Cut the butter into ½-inch cubes. Using a peeler, remove the green rind of the lime, avoiding the white pith; mince the rind to get 2 teaspoons of zest. Quarter the lime. Peel and mince the shallot.

2 Roast the carrots & tatsoi

Place the carrots on a sheet pan and drizzle with about 2 teaspoons of olive oil. Season with salt and pepper and toss to thoroughly coat. Arrange in a single, even layer and roast 10 to 12 minutes, or until browned and tender when pierced with a knife. On a separate sheet pan, season the tatsoi with salt and pepper and toss with about 2 teaspoons of olive oil. Arrange in a single, even layer and roast 6 to 7 minutes, or until browned and tender. Remove from the oven.

3 Cook the couscous

While the vegetables roast, add the couscous to the pot of boiling water. Cook 5 to 6 minutes, or until the couscous is completely tender. Drain thoroughly and return to the pot. Stir in the juice of 2 lime wedges and a drizzle of olive oil; season with salt and pepper to taste. Set aside.

4 Cook the cod

Pat the cod fillets dry and season with salt and pepper on both sides. Place the flour in a bowl. Working one at a time, completely coat each cod fillet in the flour (shaking off any excess). In a medium pan (nonstick, if you have one), heat 2 teaspoons of olive oil on medium-high until hot. Add the coated fillets and cook 4 to 5 minutes per side, or until golden brown and cooked through. Transfer to a plate. Wipe out the pan.

5 Make the makrut lime butter sauce & plate your dish

In the same pan used to cook the fish, heat 2 teaspoons of olive oil on medium-high until hot. Add the shallot; season with salt and pepper. Cook 30 seconds to 1 minute, or until slightly softened and fragrant. Add the lime zest and ¼ cup of water; turn off the heat, leaving the pan on the stove. Gradually add the butter cubes, whisking until completely combined and smooth. Stir in the juice of the remaining lime wedges and set aside. Stir the mint into the couscous. To plate your dish, divide the couscous, roasted vegetables and cod between 2 plates. Spoon the makrut lime butter sauce over the top.

The Citrus Frontier: Ripe to You

EVEN IN WINTER, the citrus groves of California's San Joaquin Valley are vivid with green. You'll find citrus of every shape and color glinting among the branches, their heft swaying gently in the temperate breeze.

It's here that Eric Christensen and his wife, Kim, have set up Ripe to You. Envisioning a new kind of farm, they eschewed the values of large-scale commercial agriculture. And they've succeeded. Eric cares deeply about the citrus he grows—so much so that his interest extends beyond the tree: "I'm interested in the history of the fruit, what it signifies, what it has meant to cultures in the past," Eric says. The wisdom of this wholesome approach is proven by the taste of his produce: it's nothing short of astounding.

To showcase the authentic ripeness of his products, each piece of citrus sold comes with a leaf attached so consumers can see the vitality and vibrancy of the fruit. But it isn't just there for show. It's a symbol of what Eric stands for. He allows every piece of fruit on his land to ripen on its own, on the tree. He'll sometimes handpick a tree at six separate times to get the best fruit. Eric is off the beaten path. He grows rare, unique varieties using traditional techniques (and a few he's dreamed up along the way).

Eric's knowledge and his eye towards the past are rare things—almost as rare as the specialty crops he grows. He sees the future for what it is and wants to pass his knowledge on to the next generation. We're happy to share his story with you.

Seared Pork Tenderloin Medallions

with Roasted Carrot, Avocado & Orange Salad over Farro

Orange supremes are orange slices with the rind, pith and membrane removed. Texturally, they're unrivaled: because the fruit's tart, sweet flavor is concentrated in the interior, you're left with nothing but fragile, delicious pulp that just barely holds itself together. The same technique can be applied to nearly any citrus fruit, and supremes can be served in countless ways. Here, you'll use them to add tang to a vegetable salad served with tasty pork medallions.

MAKES 2 SERVINGS • ABOUT 700 CALORIES PER SERVING

Ingredients

1 12-Ounce Pork Tenderloin
3-4 Sprigs Parsley
2 Sprigs Oregano
1 Lime
1 Avocado
1 Medium Carrot
1 Small Red Onion
1 Orange
⅔ Cup Semi-Pearled Farro
1 Teaspoon Hot Hungarian Paprika
1 Teaspoon Ground Cumin
1 Tablespoon Honey

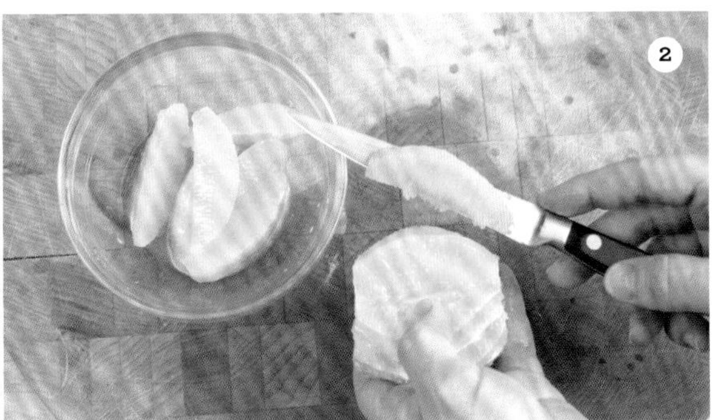

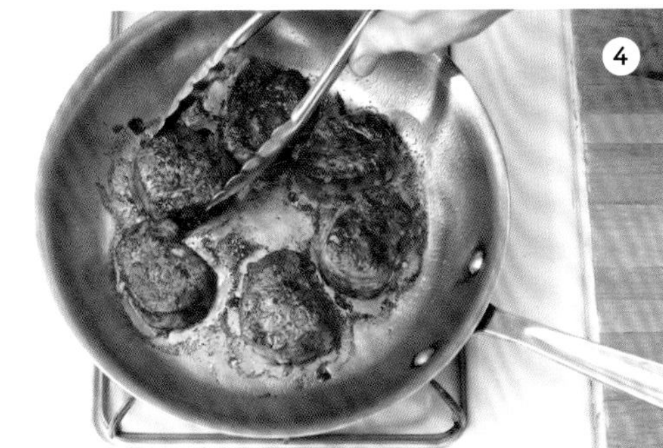

1 Prepare the ingredients

Preheat the oven to 425°F. Wash and dry the fresh produce. Heat a medium pot of salted water to boiling on high. Cut the pork tenderloin into six 1-inch-thick medallions. Pick the parsley and oregano leaves off the stems; discard the stems. Roughly chop the oregano leaves. Quarter the lime. Peel, pit and thinly slice the avocado; top with the juice of 1 lime wedge to prevent browning. Peel the carrot and cut into sticks. Peel and thinly slice the onion.

2 Make the orange supremes

Cut off the top and bottom of the orange, so it sits flat on the cutting board, then cut away the peel and white pith. Using a knife, cut out the segments (or supremes) from between the membranes and place them in a small bowl. Squeeze the juice from the leftover membranes over the orange supremes; discard the membranes.

3 Cook the farro & roast the carrots

Place the farro on a clean, dry sheet pan. Toast in the oven 4 to 6 minutes, or until lightly browned and fragrant. Once the water is boiling, add the toasted farro and cook 22 to 25 minutes, or until tender. Drain thoroughly and return to the pot. While the farro cooks, place the carrots on the same sheet pan used to toast the farro. Drizzle with olive oil and season with salt and pepper to taste; toss to thoroughly coat and arrange in a single, even layer. Roast, stirring halfway through, 10 to 12 minutes, or until tender. Remove from oven.

4 Cook the pork

After the carrots have roasted for about 5 minutes, season the pork medallions with salt and pepper, then coat with the paprika, cumin and oregano. Drizzle with a little olive oil. Using your hands, rub the seasonings into the meat. In a medium pan, heat 2 teaspoons of olive oil on medium until hot. Cook the coated pork medallions 3 to 4 minutes per side for medium, or until they reach your desired degree of doneness. Transfer the cooked pork to a plate, leaving any drippings in the pan. Add the roasted carrots to the pan and toss to coat. Set aside.

5 Finish the farro, dress the salad & plate your dish

Stir the juice from the orange supremes and 1 tablespoon of olive oil into the cooked farro; season with salt and pepper to taste. In a small bowl, combine the honey and the juice of the remaining lime wedges; season with salt and pepper. Slowly whisk in 2 tablespoons of olive oil until well combined. In a separate bowl, combine the carrots, orange supremes, avocado, onion and parsley leaves. Toss with enough of the lime-honey vinaigrette to coat the salad (you may have extra vinaigrette); season with salt and pepper to taste. To plate your dish, divide the dressed farro and pork medallions between 2 plates. Top with the salad. Garnish with any remaining vinaigrette.

Braised Moroccan-Style Salmon & Greens

with Quick-Preserved Lemon, Pine Nuts & Red Quinoa

After a lemon sits in salty brine, any bitterness in the pith and peel mellow to create preserved lemon, a condiment used in North African and Indian cuisines. The fruits cure for weeks, or even months, so that all the tartness disappears—leaving behind just their bright, citrusy flavor. In this recipe you'll make a quick version, adding brightness to the salmon after braising it in a bed of pine nuts, currants and vegetables. (You'll learn how to quick preserve in more depth on page 124.)

MAKES 2 SERVINGS • ABOUT 700 CALORIES PER SERVING

Ingredients

2 5-Ounce Skinless Salmon Fillets
3 Cloves Garlic
3-4 Sprigs Mint
1 Meyer Lemon
2 Tablespoons Granulated Sugar
1 Pound Colorful Cauliflower (Orange, Green or Purple)
½ Pound Green Kale
2 Tablespoons Capers
¾ Cup Red Quinoa
¼ Cup Pine Nuts, Raw
2 Tablespoon Dried Currants
2 Teaspoons Ras El Hanout

1 Prepare the ingredients

Wash and dry the fresh produce. Heat a medium pot of salted water to boiling on high. Remove the salmon from the refrigerator to bring to room temperature. Peel and mince the garlic. Pick the mint leaves off the stems; discard the stems. Cut the lemon in half lengthwise and remove the seeds. Thinly slice one half of the lemon (including the rind) crosswise; cut the remaining half into 2 wedges. In a small bowl, combine the sliced lemon, sugar and 1 teaspoon of salt; stir to combine. Remove and discard the core of the cauliflower; cut the head into small florets. Cut out and discard the stems of the kale; roughly chop the leaves. Roughly chop the capers.

2 Cook the quinoa

Once the water is boiling, add the quinoa. Cook 18 to 20 minutes, or until tender. Drain thoroughly and return to the pot. Stir in the juice of the lemon wedges and a drizzle of olive oil; season with salt and pepper to taste. Set aside.

3 Toast the pine nuts

While the quinoa cooks, heat a medium pan (nonstick, if you have one), on medium until hot. Add the pine nuts and cook, stirring occasionally, 3 to 4 minutes, or until golden brown and toasted. Transfer to a small bowl and set aside. Wipe out the pan.

4 Cook the cauliflower

In the same pan used to toast the pine nuts, heat 2 teaspoons of olive oil on medium-high until hot. Add the cauliflower and season with salt and pepper. Cook, stirring occasionally, 6 to 8 minutes, or until slightly browned. Transfer to a plate and set aside. Wipe out the pan.

5 Braise the salmon & plate your dish

Season the salmon with salt and pepper on both sides. In the same pan used to cook the cauliflower, heat 2 teaspoons of olive oil on medium-high until hot. Add the garlic and cook, stirring frequently, 1 to 2 minutes, or until golden brown and fragrant. Add the kale, pine nuts, currants, ras el hanout, cooked cauliflower and 1 cup of water; season with salt and pepper. Create 2 wells in the vegetables and nestle a seasoned salmon fillet into each well; tightly cover the pan with aluminum foil. Cook 7 to 9 minutes, or until the fish is cooked to your desired degree of doneness. Remove from heat. To plate your dish, divide the quinoa and vegetable mixture between 2 dishes. Top each with a piece of salmon. Stir the mint (roughly chopping the leaves just before adding) into the bowl of quick-preserved lemon. Garnish each dish with the quick-preserved lemon and a spoonful of its juices.

Pan-Seared Hanger Steaks

with "Creamed" Spinach & Lemon-Butter Purple Potatoes

Lemon and butter go together. The acidity of citrus and the smooth richness of golden cream combine to make a sophisticated sauce that's wonderful on a wide variety of dishes, from meat to fish to vegetables. In this recipe, you'll use it to finish and brown the purple potatoes. Served with "creamed" spinach made with Parmesan cheese, this meal is our homemade take on the classic steakhouse dinner.

MAKES 2 SERVINGS • ABOUT 650 CALORIES PER SERVING

Ingredients

2 5-Ounce Hanger Steaks
2 Cloves Garlic
1 Small Bunch Chives
1 Lemon
½ Pound Baby Purple Potatoes
½ Pound Spinach
2 Tablespoons Butter
¼ Teaspoon Crushed Red Pepper Flakes
3 Tablespoons Grated Parmesan Cheese

1 Prepare the ingredients & cook the potatoes

Wash and dry the fresh produce. Heat a medium pot of salted water to boiling on high. Remove the steaks from the refrigerator to bring to room temperature. Peel and mince the garlic. Mince the chives. Quarter the lemon and remove the seeds. Cut the potatoes into bite-sized pieces. Once the water is boiling, add the potatoes. Cook 8 to 10 minutes, or until tender when pierced with a fork; drain and set aside.

2 Start the spinach

While the potatoes cook, in a large pan, heat 2 teaspoons of olive oil on medium until hot. Add the spinach; season with salt and pepper. Cook, stirring frequently, 2 to 3 minutes, or until completely wilted. Remove the wilted spinach from the pan and drain thoroughly; set aside. Wipe out the pan. When cool enough to handle, finely chop the drained spinach.

3 Cook the steaks

While the spinach cools, pat the steaks dry with paper towels and season with salt and pepper on both sides. In the same pan used to cook the spinach, heat 2 teaspoons of olive oil on medium-high until hot. Add the seasoned steaks and cook, loosely covering the pan with aluminum foil, 5 to 7 minutes per side for medium-rare, or until they reach your desired degree of doneness. Transfer the cooked steaks to a plate and let rest for at least 5 minutes. Wipe out the pan.

4 Finish the potatoes

While the steaks rest, in the same pan used to cook the steaks, melt half the butter on medium-high. Add the drained potatoes and cook, tossing to coat, 1 to 2 minutes, or until lightly browned. Remove from heat; stir in the chives and the juice of 2 lemon wedges. Season with salt and pepper to taste and transfer to a plate.

5 Finish the spinach & plate your dish

In the same pan used to coat the potatoes, melt the remaining butter on medium heat. Add the garlic, as much of the crushed red pepper flakes as you'd like and the chopped spinach. Cook, stirring frequently, 30 seconds to 1 minute. Turn off the heat and add 2 tablespoons of water and the Parmesan cheese. Stir until creamy; season with salt and pepper to taste. To plate your dish, find the lines of muscle (or grain) of the steak. Thinly slice the steak crosswise against the grain. Add any steak juices from the cutting board to the spinach and stir to combine. Divide the steak, potatoes and "creamed" spinach between 2 plates. Garnish with the remaining lemon wedges.

Pan-Seared Tilapia

with Chermoula & Cucumber-Blood Orange Salad

Some things are just better with citrus. Fresh fish is one of them. Whether it's lemon or lime, tart fruit is a mainstay of pescetarian cooking. Here, you'll complement the flavor of the tilapia with blood orange supremes. Served in a side salad, blood orange brings out the citrusy, spiced flavors of chermoula, a traditional, Moroccan sauce made with cumin, coriander, sweet paprika, fresh cilantro and, most importantly, lemon.

MAKES 2 SERVINGS • ABOUT 510 CALORIES PER SERVING

Ingredients

2 6-Ounce Tilapia Fillets
10-12 Sprigs Cilantro
2 Sprigs Dill
2 Cloves Garlic
1 Lemon
1 Kirby Cucumber
1 Shallot
¾ Cup Israeli Couscous
1 Blood Orange
½ Teaspoon Ground Coriander
½ Teaspoon Ground Cumin
¼ Teaspoon Sweet Paprika

1 Prepare the ingredients

Wash and dry the fresh produce. Heat a small pot of salted water to boiling on high. Remove the tilapia from the refrigerator to bring to room temperature. Very finely chop the cilantro leaves and stems. Pick the dill off the stems; discard the stems and finely chop the leaves. Peel and mince the garlic; using the side of your knife, smash until it resembles a paste. Cut the lemon into 6 wedges; remove the seeds. Cut the cucumber in half lengthwise, then thinly slice on an angle. Peel and mince the shallot to get 2 tablespoons of minced shallot. (You may have extra shallot.)

2 Cook the Israeli couscous

Once the water is boiling, add the Israeli couscous. Cook 5 to 6 minutes, or until cooked through and tender. Drain thoroughly, rinse with warm water and return to the pot.

3 Make the supremes

While the couscous cooks, cut off about ¼ inch of the top and the bottom ends of the blood orange; sit the orange flat on a cutting board. (Only cut off enough of the top and bottom to reveal the fruit.) Following the contour of the orange, cut away and discard the peel and white pith. Over a small bowl, using a knife, cut out the individual citrus segments (or supremes) from the membranes that separate them. Place the supremes in a bowl. Squeeze the juice of the leftover membranes over the supremes; discard the membranes.

4 Make the salad & chermoula sauce

Add the cucumber, blood orange supremes, dill and as much minced shallot as you'd like (you may have extra shallot) to the cooked couscous. Stir in the juice of 1 lemon wedge and a drizzle of olive oil; season with salt and pepper to taste. Toss until well combined. In a small bowl, combine the chopped cilantro and garlic paste. Stir in the coriander, cumin, paprika and 1 tablespoon of olive oil; mix until well combined. Add the juice of 3 lemon wedges and mix until well combined; season with salt and pepper to taste.

5 Cook the fish & plate your dish

Pat the tilapia fillets dry, then season with salt and pepper on both sides. In a large pan (nonstick, if you have one), heat 2 teaspoons of olive oil on medium until hot. Add the seasoned fillets and cook 4 to 5 minutes per side, or until browned and cooked through. Transfer to a paper towel-lined plate. To plate your dish, divide the salad-couscous mixture between 2 dishes; top each with 1 fillet. Top with a couple spoonfuls of chermoula sauce and garnish with the remaining lemon wedges.

Beets

FIELD GUIDE TO BEETS

The following are some of our favorite heirloom and specialty varieties. The best place to find them is at your local farmers' market, or you can grow them yourself. The seeds are available through seed saver websites.

Chioggia: Named for a town in the lagoon of Venice in Italy. Also called "candy-stripe" for its concentric red and white rings. Matures very early and cooks relatively quickly.

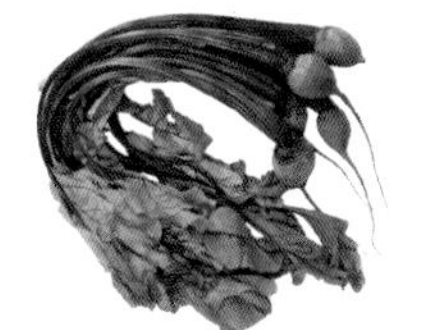

Detroit Dark Red: Heirloom variety developed in Ontario, Canada. A descendant of the blood turnip. Has one of the most reliable harvests and is one of the best beets for storage.

Early Wonder: Sweet with impressive long, green tops. The greens are often used in lieu of spinach, chard or kale. A popular, versatile variety. Named for its early availability and powerful flavor.

Formanova: Almost cylindrical in shape. An heirloom variety developed in Denmark in the late 1800s. Introduced to America shortly thereafter. Sweet and perfect for slicing. Because of its shape, generally planted in tight groups, ensuring higher yields.

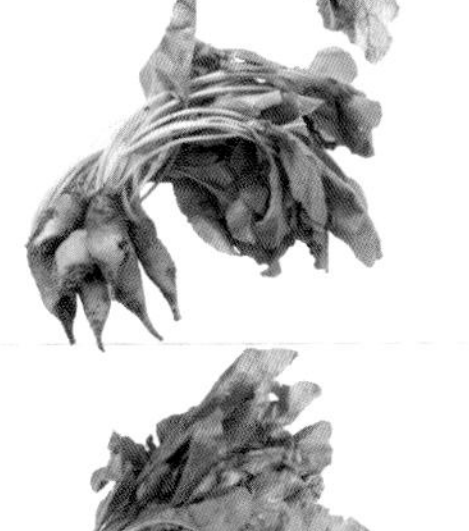

Giant Yellow Eckendorf: Huge, long, tubular root with yellow skin. Can weigh up to 20 pounds but is usually harvested at a much smaller size. Grows largely above ground.

Golden: A natural variation in which certain beet plants produce less red pigment, resulting in sweeter, golden-yellow flesh. Less earthy. Also less apt to stain your kitchen.

Sugar Beets: A pale, sweet variety with high concentrations of sucrose. Can be processed into granulated sugar. Accounts for one-fifth of the world's sugar production.

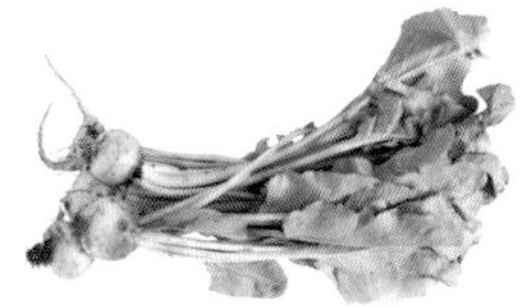

White: Sweeter and less earthy than red varieties. From the region encompassing Germany, Holland and Switzerland. Round with tasty greens.

BEETS, AND THEIR botanical cousin sugar beets, are descended from a plant called the sea beet. It was native to the sandy shores around the Mediterranean Sea and the Atlantic coast of Europe and North Africa.

Sea beets were eaten mainly for their leaves and had small, thin roots that resembled carrots. (Several subspecies of beet are still primarily cultivated for their leaves. All varieties of chard are among them.) As the sea beet was brought farther and farther inland, its root grew and became a prized vegetable.

The Oracle at Delphi, an Ancient Greek prophet who was purported to see the future, once said, "Beets are worth their weight in silver." And legend has it that Aphrodite,

the goddess of love, ate beets to retain her beauty. The beet was also commonly used in herbal remedies.

It wasn't until the 1500s that farmers began cultivating the beet into the forms we recognize today. Natural variations and selective breeding made the roots large and rounded, while retaining their almost sweet earthiness.

Beets' distinct, dark-red hue comes from a unique balance of red and yellow pigments. But new variations have continued cropping up. Yellow beets, for instance, naturally produce less of the red pigment than the yellow.

But whatever the balance—as you'll see in these recipes—beets are one of the most beautiful and delicious foods in the world.

Seared Salmon

with Arugula, Candy-Stripe Beets & Horseradish Sour Cream

It's not a dream! This beet variety, though fantastical-seeming, is real. One of our favorite things, it's called a candy-stripe, or chioggia beet, and it's a Northern Italian cultivar with gorgeous, concentric, red-and-white rings. It's especially sweet, and it doesn't stain as easily as the more common maroon beet. In this recipe, you'll use it to add satisfying earthiness to rich, seared salmon, farro and Brussels sprouts served with horseradish-spiced sour cream.

MAKES 2 SERVINGS • ABOUT 560 CALORIES PER SERVING

Ingredients

6 Ounces Candy-Stripe Beets, Without Greens
2 5-Ounce Skinless Salmon Fillets
3 Ounces Brussels Sprouts
1 1-Inch Piece Fresh Horseradish
1 Shallot
1 Tablespoon Sherry Vinegar
1 Small Bunch Chives
¾ Cup Pearled Farro
2 Ounces Arugula
¼ Cup Sour Cream

1 Cook the beets

Wash and dry the fresh produce. Heat a large pot of salted water to boiling on high. Add the beets and cook 20 to 22 minutes, or until tender when pierced with a fork; drain and set aside. When the beets are cool enough to handle, using a paper towel and your fingers, gently rub the skins off the beets; discard the skins. Peel and slice the beets into thin rounds.

2 Prepare the ingredients

While the beets cook, heat a small pot of salted water to boiling on high. Remove the salmon from the refrigerator to bring to room temperature. Cut off and discard the stem ends of the Brussels sprouts. Cut each head in half lengthwise, then thinly slice. Peel and grate the horseradish. Peel and mince the shallot to get 2 tablespoons of minced shallot; place the minced shallot in a small bowl with the sherry vinegar. Finely chop the chives.

3 Cook the farro & make the horseradish sour cream

Add the farro to the small pot of boiling water; cook 16 to 18 minutes, or until tender. Drain thoroughly and return to the pot. Add the arugula and a drizzle of olive oil. Toss gently to mix and season with salt and pepper to taste. Set aside. While the farro cooks, in a small bowl, combine the horseradish and sour cream; season with salt and pepper to taste. Set aside.

4 Cook the fish

Season the salmon fillets with salt and pepper on both sides. In a medium pan (nonstick, if you have one), heat 2 teaspoons of olive oil on medium-high until hot. Cook 2 to 3 minutes per side, or until they reach your desired degree of doneness.

5 Finish & plate your dish

In a large bowl, combine the Brussels sprouts, shallot-vinegar mixture, chives and sliced beets. Add a drizzle of olive oil and season with salt and pepper to taste. Divide the dressed farro and arugula between 2 dishes. Top each with a piece of salmon and half the salad. Garnish with the horseradish sour cream.

Beet & Barley Risotto

with Goat Cheese

Like all beets, red baby beets are slightly alkaline. That's why, when cooking them, it makes sense to balance them with something acidic. In this recipe, you'll add not only lemon, for a pleasant citrus bite, but also goat cheese, which boasts a tangy, creamy kick. This dish isn't just harmonious in flavor, though. It's amazingly beautiful. And that beauty means nutrition: the color of the beets is a result of their high antioxidant content.

MAKES 2 SERVINGS • ABOUT 650 CALORIES PER SERVING

Ingredients

3 Scallions
2 Cloves Garlic
1 Bunch Red Baby Beets, With Greens (About ¾ Pound)
1 Lemon
1 Yellow Onion
1 Cup Pearled Barley
3 Tablespoons Vegetable Demi-Glace
1 Tablespoon Butter
½ Cup Crumbled Goat Cheese

1 Prepare the ingredients

Wash and dry the fresh produce. Cut off and discard the roots of the scallions. Thinly slice the scallions on an angle, separating the white bottoms and green tops. Peel and mince the garlic. Separate the beet greens and bulbs. Roughly chop half the beet greens; discard the remaining half. Scrub the beet bulbs clean. Trim off the stems and thin roots of the beets; small dice the beets. (To avoid staining, you may want to wear gloves and use a plastic cutting board.) Using a peeler, remove the yellow rind of the lemon, avoiding the white pith; mince the rind to get 2 teaspoons of zest. Quarter the lemon and remove the seeds. Peel and small dice the onion.

2 Start the risotto

In a medium pot, heat 2 teaspoons of olive oil on medium until hot. Add the onion and garlic; season with salt and pepper. Cook, stirring occasionally, 3 to 4 minutes, or until softened. Stir in the barley, diced beets and lemon zest; season with salt and pepper. Cook, stirring frequently, 1 to 2 minutes, or until the barley is toasted and fragrant.

3 Add the liquids

Stir the vegetable demi-glace and 3 cups of water into the pot of vegetables; season with salt and pepper. Increase the heat to high and bring the mixture to a boil. Once boiling, reduce the heat to medium-low and simmer, stirring occasionally, 16 to 18 minutes, or until the beets and barley are tender when pierced with a fork. (If the mixture sticks to the bottom of the pot or looks dry, add up to an additional ¼ cup of water.)

4 Add the beet greens & butter

Just before the barley and beets are fully cooked through and some liquid still remains in the pot, stir in the chopped beet greens and butter. Season with salt and pepper. Cook, stirring occasionally, 1 to 2 minutes, or until the butter has melted and the beet greens have wilted. Remove from heat.

5 Finish & plate your dish

Stir the white parts of the scallions, half the goat cheese and the juice of 2 lemon wedges into the risotto. Mix until thoroughly incorporated and season with salt and pepper to taste. Divide the risotto between 2 dishes. Garnish with the green parts of the scallions, remaining goat cheese and remaining lemon wedges.

Brined Pork Chops

with Formanova Beet, Heirloom Carrot & Hazelnut Salad

Formanova beets are an heirloom variety from Denmark. They're also called "Butter Slicer" and "Cylindra" for their wonderful texture and long, cylindrical shape. Like their red beet kin, they're a lovely, dark shade of crimson. Here, their complexity completes the profile of the tender, brined pork and resonates with the earthiness of carrots and hazelnuts. Winter, nice to have you back.

MAKES 2 SERVINGS • ABOUT 615 CALORIES PER SERVING

Ingredients
4 Cloves Garlic
4 Sprigs Mint
3 Tablespoons Roasted Hazelnuts
1 Shallot
1 Tablespoon Champagne Vinegar
½ Pound Multicolored Heirloom Carrots, With Greens
½ Pound Formanova Beets, Without Greens (About 8 Ounces)
3-4 Sprigs Thyme
2 6-Ounce Center-Cut, Boneless Pork Chops
3 Tablespoons Butter

1 Prepare the ingredients & brine the pork

Wash and dry the fresh produce. Heat a large pot of salted water to boiling on high. Peel and smash the garlic cloves. Pick the mint leaves off the stems; discard the stems. Roughly chop the hazelnuts. Peel and mince the shallot to get 2 tablespoons of minced shallot; place the minced shallot in a bowl with the vinegar. Separate the carrots from the greens; reserve one-third of the greens and discard the remaining greens. Peel and slice the beets into ½-inch rounds on a paper towel-lined cutting board. In a large bowl, combine 2 of the crushed garlic cloves, half the thyme sprigs, 2 tablespoons of salt and 2 cups of warm water. Submerge the pork chops in the liquid and brine for at least 15 minutes.

2 Cook & marinate the beets

Once the water is boiling, add the beets. Cook 16 to 18 minutes, or until tender when pierced with a fork. Drain thoroughly and toss with the shallot-vinegar mixture; season with salt and pepper to taste.

3 Cook the carrots

While the beets cook, in a large pan (nonstick, if you have one), heat 2 teaspoons of olive oil on medium-high until hot. Add the carrots and cook, stirring occasionally, 4 to 6 minutes, or until slightly browned. Add 1 tablespoon of butter and ½ cup of water; season with salt and pepper. Cook, stirring occasionally, 6 to 8 minutes, or until the water has evaporated and the carrots are tender. Season with salt and pepper to taste and transfer to a bowl. Wipe out the pan.

4 Cook the pork

Remove the pork from the brine; discard the brine. Pat the pork dry with paper towels and season with salt and pepper on both sides. In the same pan used to cook the carrots, heat 2 teaspoons of olive oil on medium-high until hot. Add the seasoned pork and cook 4 to 6 minutes on the first side. Turn the pork over and cook 2 to 3 minutes. Add the remaining smashed garlic, thyme and butter. Cook, occasionally tipping the pan and spooning the melted butter over the chops, 1 to 2 minutes, or until the butter is browned and fragrant. Transfer the pork to a plate, leaving any drippings (or fond) in the pan; set the pork aside in a warm place. Let rest for at least 5 minutes. Remove and discard the garlic.

5 Finish & plate your dish

Add the carrots, hazelnuts and marinated beets to the pan of reserved fond. Cook on medium heat, stirring occasionally, 1 to 2 minutes, or until warmed through; season with salt and pepper to taste. Remove from heat and add the carrot greens and mint (thinly slicing just before adding). Slice the pork into ½-inch pieces. Divide the salad and pork between 2 dishes. Top with a couple spoonfuls of the sauce from the pan.

Chicken Schnitzel

with Watercress, Apple, Golden Beet & Walnut Salad

Beets don't have to be red to be delicious! Yellow beets, also called golden beets, are a tasty way to mix things up. Like other varieties, yellow beets have beautiful, swirling rings on the inside—just with sun-like hues of gold and orange. In our recipe for chicken schnitzel, you'll feature them in a winter salad with watercress, apples, celery and walnuts.

MAKES 2 SERVINGS • ABOUT 700 CALORIES PER SERVING

Ingredients

5 Ounces Golden Baby Beets, Without Greens
1 Meyer Lemon
1 Granny Smith Apple
1 Stalk Celery
3 Tablespoons Walnuts, Shelled & Raw
1 Shallot
1 Tablespoon Sherry Vinegar
¼ Cup Smooth Dijon Mustard
1 Cup Panko Breadcrumbs
2 6-Ounce Chicken Cutlets
3 Ounces Watercress

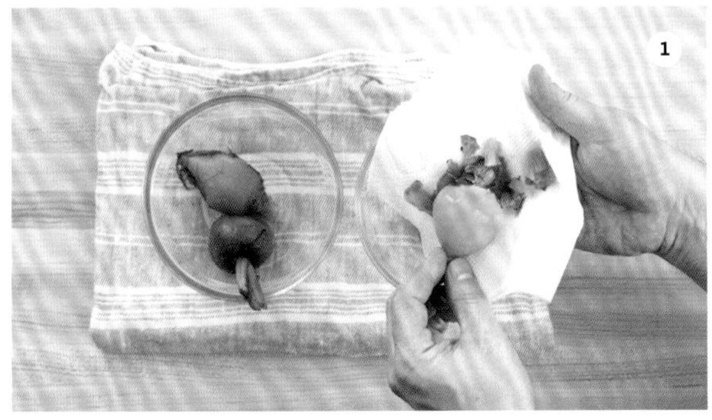

1 Cook & peel the beets

Wash and dry the fresh produce. Heat a medium pot of salted water to boiling on high. Add the beets and cook 23 to 25 minutes, or until tender when pierced with a knife. Drain thoroughly and set aside to cool slightly. When the beets are cool enough to handle, using a paper towel and your fingers, gently rub the skins off the beets; discard the skins. Cut each beet into wedges.

2 Prepare the ingredients

While the beets cook, quarter the lemon and remove the seeds. Core and cut the apple into matchsticks; toss with the juice of 2 lemon wedges to prevent browning. Thinly slice the celery on an angle. Roughly chop the walnuts. Peel and mince the shallot; place in a small bowl with the sherry vinegar and 1 teaspoon of Dijon mustard. In a large bowl, combine the remaining Dijon mustard with ¼ cup of water.

3 Toast the walnuts

Heat a medium, dry pan (nonstick, if you have one) on medium-high until hot. Add the walnuts and cook, stirring frequently, 2 to 4 minutes, or until slightly browned and fragrant. Transfer to a bowl and set aside. Wipe out the pan.

4 Bread & cook the chicken

While the beets continue to cook, place the panko breadcrumbs in a shallow bowl or on a plate. Season the chicken cutlets with salt and pepper on both sides. Working one at a time, dip each cutlet into the mustard-water mixture (shaking off the excess), then thoroughly coat in the panko breadcrumbs (letting the excess fall off). Transfer to a plate. Repeat with the remaining cutlet. In the same pan used to toast the walnuts, heat 2 teaspoons of olive oil on medium-high until hot. Add the breaded cutlets and cook 4 to 5 minutes per side, or until golden brown, crispy on the outside and cooked through.

5 Dress the salad & plate your dish

Whisk 2 tablespoons of olive oil into the vinegar-shallot-mustard mixture; season with salt and pepper to taste. In a large bowl, combine the beets, apples, toasted walnuts, celery, watercress and as much of the dressing as you'd like (you may have extra dressing); season with salt and pepper to taste. Toss gently to mix. To plate your dish, divide the chicken cutlets between 2 plates and top each with the salad. Garnish with the remaining lemon wedges.

Warm Grain Salad

with Beets, Orange, Avocado & Gorgonzola

Earthy, hearty beets need company. That's why this seasonal salad features spelt, an ancient type of wheat first grown nearly 9,000 years ago in the Middle East. It was the wheat used to make bread throughout Europe until it was replaced with the modern wheat we know today. Here, its nutty flavor goes beautifully with bright citrus, tasty gorgonzola cheese and, of course, lovely red baby beets.

MAKES 2 SERVINGS • ABOUT 575 CALORIES PER SERVING

Ingredients

3-4 Sprigs Tarragon
2-3 Radishes, Without Greens
1 Avocado
2 Tablespoons Red Wine Vinegar
1 Orange
1 Shallot
½ Cup Spelt
5-6 Red Baby Beets, Without Greens (About ¾ Pound)
¼ Cup Crumbled Gorgonzola Cheese

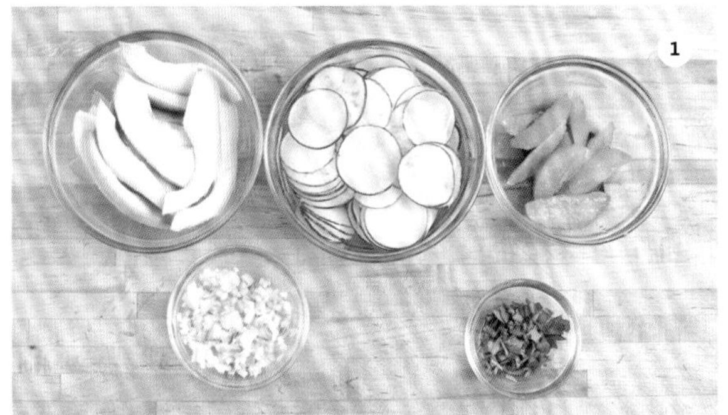

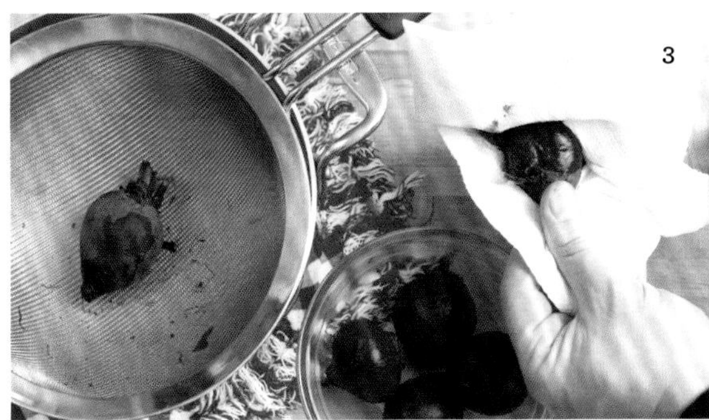

1 Prepare the ingredients

Wash and dry the fresh produce. Heat a medium pot of salted water to boiling on high. Pick the tarragon leaves off the stems; discard the stems and roughly chop the leaves. Thinly slice the radishes and place in a bowl of cold water. Pit, peel and thinly slice the avocado; toss with a splash of red wine vinegar to prevent browning. Cut away and discard the rind and white pith of the orange. Then, using a small knife, cut out segments (or supremes) from between the membranes. Place the supremes in a bowl. Squeeze the juice of the leftover membranes over the segments; discard the membranes. Peel and mince the shallot to get 2 tablespoons of minced shallot. Place the minced shallot in a small bowl with the remaining red wine vinegar.

2 Cook the spelt

Once the water is boiling, add the spelt. Cook 30 to 35 minutes, or until tender. Drain thoroughly and return to the pot.

3 Cook the beets

Place the beets in a medium pot of water. Heat to boiling on high. Once boiling, cook 20 to 22 minutes, or until tender when pierced with a knife. Drain thoroughly. When cool enough to handle, using paper towels and your hands, gently rub the skins off of the beets; discard the skins. (To avoid staining, you may want to wear gloves and use a plastic cutting board.) Cut the beets into wedges and place in a bowl.

4 Make the vinaigrette

While the beets and spelt cook, season the shallot-vinegar mixture with salt and pepper. Slowly whisk in 2 tablespoons of olive oil until combined.

5 Finish & plate your dish

Add some of the vinaigrette to the beets and toss to thoroughly coat. Add the radishes, tarragon and orange supremes (including the juice from the bowl). Add some of the remaining vinaigrette (you may have extra vinaigrette) to the cooked spelt. Season with salt and pepper to taste and toss to coat. To plate your dish, divide the dressed spelt between 2 dishes. Top the spelt with the dressed beets and avocado. Garnish with the crumbled gorgonzola cheese.

Fresh Beet Pasta

with Swiss Chard, Goat Cheese & Walnuts

The Swiss are known for many things: chocolate, neutrality, fine watches and delicious chard. Well, not really. The vegetable itself isn't native to Switzerland: it gets its name from the 19th-Century Swiss botanist who first scientifically documented it. In this recipe, we've paired chard with delicious, red beet pasta. Why? Because beets and chard are vegetable siblings, both descended from the same plant. Their complementary flavors provide an earthy counterpoint to tangy goat cheese and toasted walnuts.

MAKES 2 SERVINGS • ABOUT 700 CALORIES PER SERVING

Ingredients

3 Cloves Garlic
1 Lemon
½ Pound Red Beets
1 Yellow Onion
¾ Pound Swiss Chard
¼ Cup Walnuts, Shelled & Raw
½ Pound Fresh Beet Linguine Pasta
2 Tablespoons Butter, Salted
½ Cup Crumbled Goat Cheese

1 Prepare the ingredients

Wash and dry the fresh produce. Heat a large pot of salted water to boiling on high. Peel and mince the garlic. Using a peeler, remove the yellow rind of the lemon, avoiding the white pith; mince the rind to get 2 teaspoons of zest. Quarter the lemon and remove the seeds. Peel and small dice the beets and onion. Separate the chard leaves from the stems; roughly chop the leaves and thinly slice the stems, keeping them separate. Roughly chop the walnuts.

2 Toast the walnuts

Heat a large, dry pan on medium-high until hot. Add the walnuts and toast, stirring frequently, 1 to 3 minutes, or until lightly browned and fragrant. Transfer to a small bowl and set aside. Wipe out the pan.

3 Cook the vegetables

In the same pan used to toast the walnuts, heat 2 teaspoons of olive oil on high until hot. Add the beets and season with salt and pepper. Cook, stirring occasionally, 4 to 5 minutes, or until the beets have softened slightly. Add the onion and garlic; season with salt and pepper. (If the pan looks dry, add an additional teaspoon of olive oil.) Cook, stirring frequently, 4 to 6 minutes, or until the vegetables have softened. Add the chard stems; season with salt and pepper. Cook, stirring occasionally, 2 to 3 minutes, or until softened. Stir in the chard leaves and lemon zest; season with salt and pepper. Cook, stirring occasionally, 2 to 3 minutes, or until the leaves have wilted. Remove from heat and set aside.

4 Cook the pasta

Add the linguine to the pot of boiling water and cook 3 to 4 minutes, or until just shy of al dente. Drain the pasta, reserving about 1 cup of the pasta cooking water; transfer the pasta directly to the pan of vegetables.

5 Finish & plate your dish

Heat the pan of vegetables and pasta on medium; add the butter, the juice of 2 lemon wedges, half the toasted walnuts and ½ cup of reserved pasta water. Cook, stirring frequently, 2 to 4 minutes, or until the pasta absorbs the liquid. (If the pasta looks dry, add up to an additional ½ cup of pasta cooking water to achieve your desired consistency.) Season with salt and pepper to taste; remove from heat. To plate your dish, divide the pasta between 2 plates. Garnish with the goat cheese, remaining toasted walnuts and remaining lemon wedges.

Cabbage

FIELD GUIDE TO CABBAGE

The following are some of our favorite heirloom and specialty varieties. The best place to find them is at your local farmers' market, or you can grow them yourself. The seeds are available through seed saver websites.

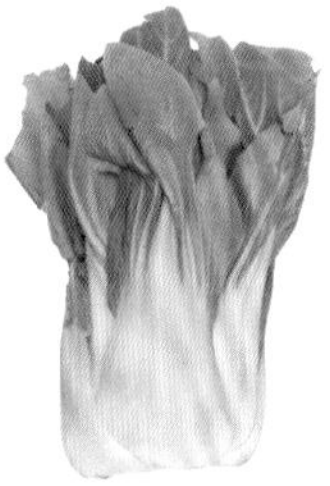

Bok Choy: Means, literally, "white vegetable" in Cantonese. Native to the Yangtze River Delta in China. Prized in the Ming Dynasty for its medicinal properties.

Kohlrabi: A curious variety of cabbage with few leaves and a large, spherical stem. Cultivated extensively in Germany. "Kohlrabi" in German means "cabbage turnip."

Cannonball Cabbage: Large, dense heads of closely packed, pale leaves. One of the more common kinds of cabbage found in grocery stores.

Michihili: A loose-leaf form of Chinese cabbage. A tender, mild variety often used raw in salads. First cultivated in the 14th Century.

Choy Sum: In Cantonese, means "vegetable heart." Also called "Chinese flowering cabbage" for its bright yellow, oval-petaled flowers. Over 30 varieties are cultivated in mainland China.

Napa Cabbage: Gets its name from the Japanese word "nappa," which is used to refer to the edible leaves of any plant. Has been cultivated in Asia since the 14th Century.

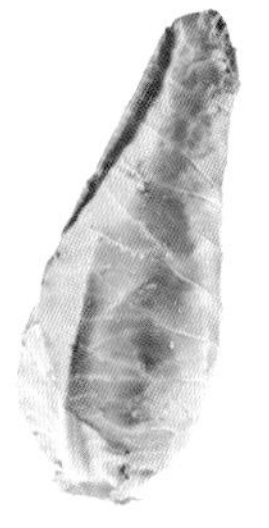

Cone Cabbage: Appears in early winter. Known for its conical shape. Native to Filder, Germany. Specifically bred for the colder regions of Europe.

Red Drumhead Cabbage: A strain of a large, Dutch variety. Characterized by its flat top and round middle.

January King Cabbage: Has been cultivated in England since 1867. Its blue-green leaves are blushed with purple at the edges. Will tolerate extremely cold weather and even grow through snow.

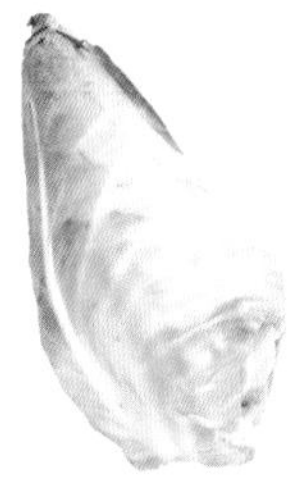

Winnigstadt Cabbage: Distinguished by bluish-green conical heads and tender leaves. First introduced to the U.S. in 1866 by a seed company in Marblehead, Massachusetts.

CABBAGE IS BY far the oldest cultivated vegetable in the *brassica* family. It was prized by the Egyptians, touted by the Greeks and Romans and spread throughout the world. The list of common culinary vegetables descended from cabbage is staggering. Cauliflower, broccoli, kale and Brussels sprouts can all trace their lineage back to the same wild ancestor.

However, history's first cabbages would be nearly unrecognizable to us. They were spindly plants that grew on the rocky shelves of seaside cliffs. (The plant's ability to tolerate salt helped it dominate these areas.)

These cabbages also lacked the signature large head that is commonplace today. In form, ancient cabbages looked more like kale than anything

else. The head was originally just a central bud that grew on a long stalk.

Domestication and selective cultivation gave rise to the hearty, modern-day cabbage and its relatives. Cabbages that were cultivated for their sizeable outer leaves became kale. Others, cultivated for their flowering stalks, became broccoli. Around the 1st Century, the first true "headed" cabbages began popping up around the globe.

Farmers purposefully bred cabbage for their central bud, and it became larger and larger, eventually becoming the tender, delicious majority of the plant we know it as today. And, though there is an array of cabbages available on the market, most of what we eat is that central bud, the tight crush of flower petals, turned inward.

Salmon Pastrami on Rye

with Red Cabbage & Green Apple Slaw

Cabbage has dozens of traditional preparations. One of these is coleslaw: shredded raw cabbage, usually marinated in a vinaigrette. Here, you'll make your slaw with green apple and red cabbage, then serve it alongside a New York City classic: the pastrami sandwich with Thousand Island dressing. But wait! Instead of pastrami, you'll use delicious salmon, seasoning it with a blend of brown sugar, coriander, ground mustard and paprika. You may never have to go to the deli again.

MAKES 2 SERVINGS • ABOUT 700 CALORIES PER SERVING

Ingredients

3 Cornichons
1 Lemon
1 Granny Smith Apple
¼ Head Red Cabbage
1 Teaspoon Ground Coriander
1 Teaspoon Ground Black Pepper
½ Teaspoon Light Brown Sugar
½ Teaspoon Sweet Paprika
¼ Teaspoon Ground Black Mustard Seed
2 6-Ounce Skinless Salmon Fillets
1 Tablespoon Honey
1 Tablespoon Whole Grain Dijon Mustard
2 Tablespoons Mayonnaise
1 Tablespoon Ketchup
4 Slices Rye Bread
1 Cup Sauerkraut

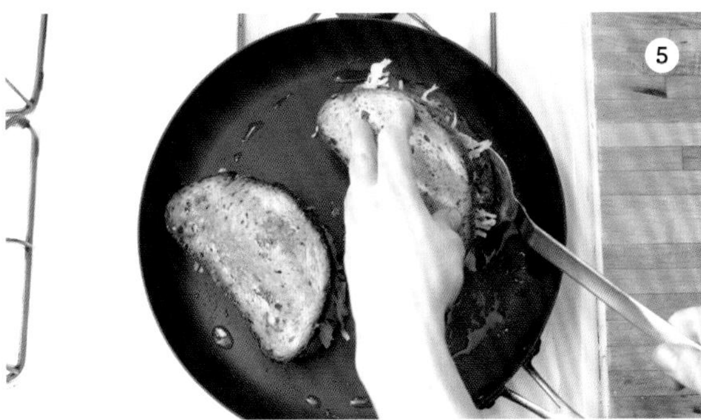

1 Prepare the ingredients

Wash and dry the fresh produce. Finely chop the cornichons. Quarter the lemon and remove the seeds. Core the apple and cut it into thin matchsticks; toss with the juice of 1 lemon wedge to prevent browning. Cut out and discard the core of the cabbage; thinly slice the leaves. In a small bowl, combine the coriander, black pepper, light brown sugar, paprika and mustard seeds to create a spice blend. Season the salmon fillets with a little salt, then thoroughly coat with the spice blend.

2 Make the lemon vinaigrette & marinate the cabbage

In a small bowl, combine the honey, whole grain Dijon mustard and the juice of 2 lemon wedges; season with salt and pepper. Slowly whisk in 2 tablespoons of olive oil until well combined. In a medium bowl, season the red cabbage with salt and pepper and toss with enough of the vinaigrette to thoroughly coat the cabbage (you may have extra vinaigrette). Set aside to marinate.

3 Cook the salmon

In a medium pan (nonstick, if you have one), heat 2 teaspoons of olive oil on medium until hot. Add the coated salmon fillets and cook, loosely covering the pan with aluminum foil, 4 to 6 minutes per side, or until they reach your desired degree of doneness. Transfer the cooked salmon to a plate and let rest for at least 5 minutes. Wipe out the pan.

4 Make the dressing & assemble the sandwiches

While the salmon cools, make the Thousand Island dressing. In a small bowl, combine the mayonnaise, ketchup, cornichons and the juice of the remaining lemon wedge. Lay the rye bread slices out on a work surface and spread each with a layer of Thousand Island dressing. Using a fork or your hands, break the cooked salmon fillets into large pieces; divide the salmon pieces between 2 of the bread slices. Top each with the sauerkraut and another slice of bread to complete the sandwiches.

5 Grill the sandwiches & plate your dish

In the same pan used to cook the fish, heat 2 teaspoons of olive oil on medium until hot. Add the sandwiches and cook 3 to 5 minutes per side, or until browned. (If the pan seems dry, add another teaspoon of olive oil after flipping the sandwiches.) To plate your dish, stir the apple into the dressed red cabbage. Cut the sandwiches in half. Divide the grilled sandwiches and cabbage slaw between 2 plates.

Fresh Gnocchi

with Sausage & Savoy Cabbage

Savoy is a mild, earthy cabbage variety. It has the same shape as green cabbage—a tightly wrapped ball of leaves—but its leaves have an amazing, crinkly texture. They also vary in hue, from chartreuse to a dark, almost bluish green. In this recipe, you'll cook the Savoy with red wine vinegar to lend it sharpness and kick, then pair it with rich, sweet Italian sausage, Parmesan and tender gnocchi dumplings.

MAKES 2 SERVINGS • ABOUT 600 CALORIES PER SERVING

Ingredients

8 Ounces Sweet Italian Sausage
3 Cloves Garlic
1 Small Red Onion
½ Head Savoy Cabbage
¼ Teaspoon Crushed Red Pepper Flakes
1 Tablespoon Red Wine Vinegar
8 Ounces Gnocchi
¼ Cup Grated Parmesan Cheese

1 Prepare the ingredients

Wash and dry the fresh produce. Heat a large pot of salted water to boiling on high. Remove the sausage from the casing and break it into small pieces; discard the casing. Peel and thinly slice the garlic and onion. Cut out and discard the core of the cabbage; thinly slice the leaves.

2 Cook the sausage

In a large pan (nonstick, if you have one), heat 1 teaspoon of olive oil on medium-high until hot. Add the sausage and cook, breaking the sausage apart with a spoon, 3 to 5 minutes, or until browned.

3 Add the aromatics

Once the sausage is browned, add the onion, garlic and as much of the crushed red pepper flakes as you'd like, depending on how spicy you'd like the dish to be. Season with salt and pepper. Cook, stirring occasionally, 3 to 5 minutes, or until the vegetables have softened.

4 Add the cabbage

Add the cabbage to the pan of sausage and aromatics; season with salt and pepper. Cook, stirring occasionally, 6 to 8 minutes, or until the cabbage has wilted. Stir in the red wine vinegar and remove from heat.

5 Cook the gnocchi & plate your dish

Add the gnocchi to the pot of boiling water. Cook 2 to 3 minutes, or until the gnocchi float to the top of the pot. Reserve 1 cup of the water used to cook the pasta. Using a slotted spoon or strainer, transfer the cooked gnocchi directly to the pan of sausage and vegetables. Add all but a pinch of the Parmesan cheese and ½ cup of reserved pasta water. Cook on medium-high for 1 to 2 minutes, or until thoroughly combined; season with salt and pepper to taste. (If desired, slowly add the remaining reserved pasta water to achieve your desired consistency.) Remove from heat. To plate your dish, divide the gnocchi between 2 bowls. Garnish with the remaining Parmesan cheese.

Chicken Mulligatawny Soup

with Kohlrabi & Basmati Rice

Kohlrabi is a vegetable in the cabbage family. Its name is derived from the Austrian term "kohlrübe," meaning, literally, "cabbage turnip," because of its turnip-like bulb with greens on top. Here, we're saluting its mild, crisp flavor and texture by featuring it in mulligatawny, an Anglo-Indian soup. Spiced to perfection and topped with toasted coconut, this rice-and-chicken meal is a warming hearth in winter.

MAKES 2 SERVINGS • ABOUT 580 CALORIES PER SERVING

Ingredients

5-6 Sprigs Cilantro
1 Medium Kohlrabi, Without Greens
1 Carrot
1 Red Onion
1 Lime
2 Teaspoons Whole Black Mustard Seeds
2 Teaspoons Whole Fenugreek Seeds
1 Teaspoon Ground Coriander
½ Teaspoon Cayenne Pepper
½ Teaspoon Curry Powder
½ Teaspoon Ground Ginger
½ Teaspoon Ground Turmeric
1 Tablespoon Ghee
¾ Cup Basmati Rice
¼ Cup Unsweetened Coconut Flakes
2 Boneless, Skinless Chicken Thighs
3 Tablespoons Golden Raisins
1 13.5-Ounce Can Light Coconut Milk

1

2

3

4

5

1 **Prepare the ingredients**
Wash and dry the fresh produce. Pick the cilantro leaves off the stems; discard the stems. Halve the kohlrabi lengthwise; cut each half into small wedges. Peel and thinly slice the carrot into rounds. Peel and thinly slice the onion. Using a peeler, remove the green rind of the lime, avoiding the white pith; mince the rind to get 2 teaspoons of zest. Quarter the lime.

2 **Make the spice blend & cook the rice**
In a small bowl, combine the mustard seeds, fenugreek seeds, coriander, cayenne pepper, curry powder, ginger and turmeric to create a spice blend. Set aside. In a medium pot, heat half the ghee and 2 teaspoons of olive oil on medium-high until hot. Add the lime zest and a big pinch of the spice blend and cook, stirring frequently, 1 to 2 minutes, or until fragrant and the seeds begin to pop. Add the basmati rice, a big pinch of salt and 1½ cups of water. Bring the mixture to a boil. Cover and reduce the heat to low. Cook 13 to 15 minutes, or until all of the liquid is absorbed and the rice is tender. Fluff the finished rice with a fork.

3 **Toast the coconut**
Heat a large pot on medium until hot. Add the coconut flakes and toast, stirring frequently, 3 to 4 minutes, or until golden brown and crunchy. Transfer to a small bowl and set aside. Wipe out the pot.

4 **Brown the chicken**
Cut the chicken into ½-inch-thick pieces. Season the chicken with salt and pepper. In the same pot used to toast the coconut, heat 2 teaspoons of oil on high until hot. Add the seasoned chicken and cook, stirring occasionally, 3 to 5 minutes, or until cooked through. Transfer to a bowl, leaving any browned bits (or fond) in the pot. Set aside.

5 **Make the soup & plate your dish**
Add 2 teaspoons of olive oil to the pot of reserved fond. Heat on medium-high until hot. Add the remaining ghee and spice blend. Cook, stirring frequently, 30 seconds to 1 minute, or until toasted and fragrant. Add the carrot, kohlrabi, celery and onion; season with salt and pepper. Cook, stirring occasionally, 3 to 5 minutes, or until the vegetables are tender. Reduce the heat to medium and add the golden raisins, cooked chicken (along with any juices on the plate), coconut milk and 1 cup of water. Simmer, stirring occasionally, 12 to 14 minutes, or until slightly thickened. Remove from heat and stir in the juice of all 4 lime wedges. To plate your dish, divide the rice and soup between 2 bowls. Garnish with the cilantro and toasted coconut.

Chile-Rubbed Flat Iron Steaks

with Quick Kimchi & Tomato Rice

In this recipe, we're following cabbage to Korea. Kimchi is Korea's national dish, and it's typically made with fermented cabbage. When fermented, cabbage has a spicy-sweet-sour flavor combination. But fermentation takes months! In this recipe, we'll give you a shortcut. The "quick kimchi" you'll marinate is bright and vinegary—the perfect topping for spice-rubbed steaks.

MAKES 2 SERVINGS • ABOUT 510 CALORIES PER SERVING

Ingredients

2 5-Ounce Flat Iron Steaks
2 Cloves Garlic
1 2-Inch Piece Ginger
2 Sprigs Basil
1 Scallion
¼ Head Napa Cabbage
¾ Cup Brown Rice
¼ Cup Rice Vinegar, Unseasoned
1 Tablespoon Granulated Sugar
1 Tablespoon Sriracha
2 Teaspoons Gochugaru (Korean Chile Flakes)
1 8-Ounce Can Tomato Sauce
1 Tablespoon Sesame Oil

1 Prepare the ingredients

Wash and dry the fresh produce. Remove the steak from the refrigerator to bring to room temperature. Peel and mince the garlic and ginger. Pick the basil leaves off the stems; discard the stems. Remove and discard the roots of the scallion. Thinly slice the scallion. Cut out and discard the core of the napa cabbage; thinly slice the leaves.

2 Cook the rice

In a small pot, combine the rice, 1½ cups of water and a pinch of salt. Heat to boiling on high. Once boiling, cover, reduce the heat to low and simmer 25 to 30 minutes, or until the rice is cooked through and the water is absorbed.

3 Make the quick kimchi

While the rice cooks, in a small bowl, combine the napa cabbage, rice vinegar, sugar, half the ginger, half the garlic and half the scallion. Stir in as much of the sriracha as you'd like, depending on how spicy you'd like the kimchi to be; season with salt and pepper to taste. Toss to coat and let stand for at least 10 minutes to marinate.

4 Cook the steaks

After the rice has cooked for about 10 minutes, season the steaks with salt and as much of the gochugaru as you'd like, depending on how spicy you'd like the steak to be. In a medium pan, heat 2 teaspoons of oil on medium-high until hot. Add the seasoned steaks and cook 3 to 4 minutes per side for medium-rare, or until they reach your desired degree of doneness. Transfer to a plate or cutting board, leaving any drippings in the pan. Loosely cover the steaks with aluminum foil to keep warm. Let rest for at least 5 minutes.

5 Finish & plate your dish

While the steaks rest, add the sesame oil to the pan of reserved steak drippings and heat on medium until hot. Add the remaining garlic, ginger and scallion and cook, stirring frequently, 30 seconds to 1 minute, or until softened. Add the cooked rice, tomato sauce and half the basil (roughly chopping just before adding); season with salt and pepper. Bring the mixture to a simmer and cook, stirring occasionally, 1 to 2 minutes, or until heated through. Remove from heat. To plate your dish, cut each steak in half. Add any steak juices from the cutting board to the rice and stir to combine. Divide the finished rice and steak between 2 plates; top with the kimchi. Spoon any extra marinade from the kimchi over the steak and rice. Garnish with the remaining basil.

Pan-Roasted Bratwurst

with Sweet and Sour Red Cabbage & Crispy Potatoes

In this recipe, you'll warm things up with sweet and sour red cabbage cooked in homemade caramel, allspice, cinnamon and nutmeg, then topped with bright parsley and red wine vinegar. There's nothing more toothsome when served up with classic German brats and potatoes cooked twice for extra crispiness. It's a warming Bavarian meal that's perfect for winter.

MAKES 2 SERVINGS • ABOUT 650 CALORIES PER SERVING

Ingredients

2 Pre-Cooked Bratwurst Sausages
3-4 Sprigs Parsley
1 Pound Russet Potatoes
½ Head Red Cabbage
¼ Cup Granulated Sugar
¾ Teaspoon Ground Allspice
¾ Teaspoon Ground Cinnamon
½ Teaspoon Ground Nutmeg
2 Tablespoons Red Wine Vinegar
2 Tablespoons Whole Grain Dijon Mustard

1 Prepare the ingredients
Preheat the oven to 475°F. Wash and dry the fresh produce. Heat a large pot of salted water to boiling on high. Remove the bratwurst from the refrigerator to bring to room temperature. Pick the parsley leaves off the stems; discard the stems and roughly chop the leaves. Peel and large dice the potatoes. Cut out and discard the core of the cabbage; thinly slice the leaves.

2 Boil & roast the potatoes
Once the pot of water is boiling, add the potatoes. Cook 5 to 6 minutes, or until tender on the outside but firm in the center when pierced with a knife. Drain the potatoes and place on a sheet pan. Drizzle the boiled potatoes with olive oil and season with salt and pepper. Toss to thoroughly coat and arrange in a single, even layer. Roast, stirring halfway through, 25 to 30 minutes, or until browned and crispy.

3 Make the caramel
While the potatoes roast, in a medium pot, heat the sugar on medium-high. Cook, without stirring, 3 to 4 minutes. (The sugar will melt, then thicken and become light amber in color.) Continue cooking the sugar until it becomes a reddish-brown color. (The caramel will continue to cook in the pot, so be ready to begin the next step almost immediately.)

4 Cook the cabbage
Carefully stir the cabbage into the pot of caramel; season with salt and pepper. Cook, stirring occasionally, 1 to 2 minutes, or until well combined. Stir in the allspice, cinnamon and nutmeg; season with salt and pepper. Reduce the heat to medium-low. Cook, stirring occasionally, 22 to 25 minutes, or until the cabbage has cooked down and is dark purple in color. Remove from heat and stir in the red wine vinegar and parsley; season with salt and pepper to taste.

5 Cook the bratwursts & plate your dish
While the potatoes and cabbage cook, in a medium pan, heat 1 teaspoon of olive oil on medium until hot. Add the bratwursts and cook, loosely covering the pan with aluminum foil, 2 to 4 minutes per side, or until golden brown and heated through. Remove from heat. To plate your dish, divide the cabbage, potatoes and bratwursts between 2 plates. Garnish with the whole grain Dijon mustard.

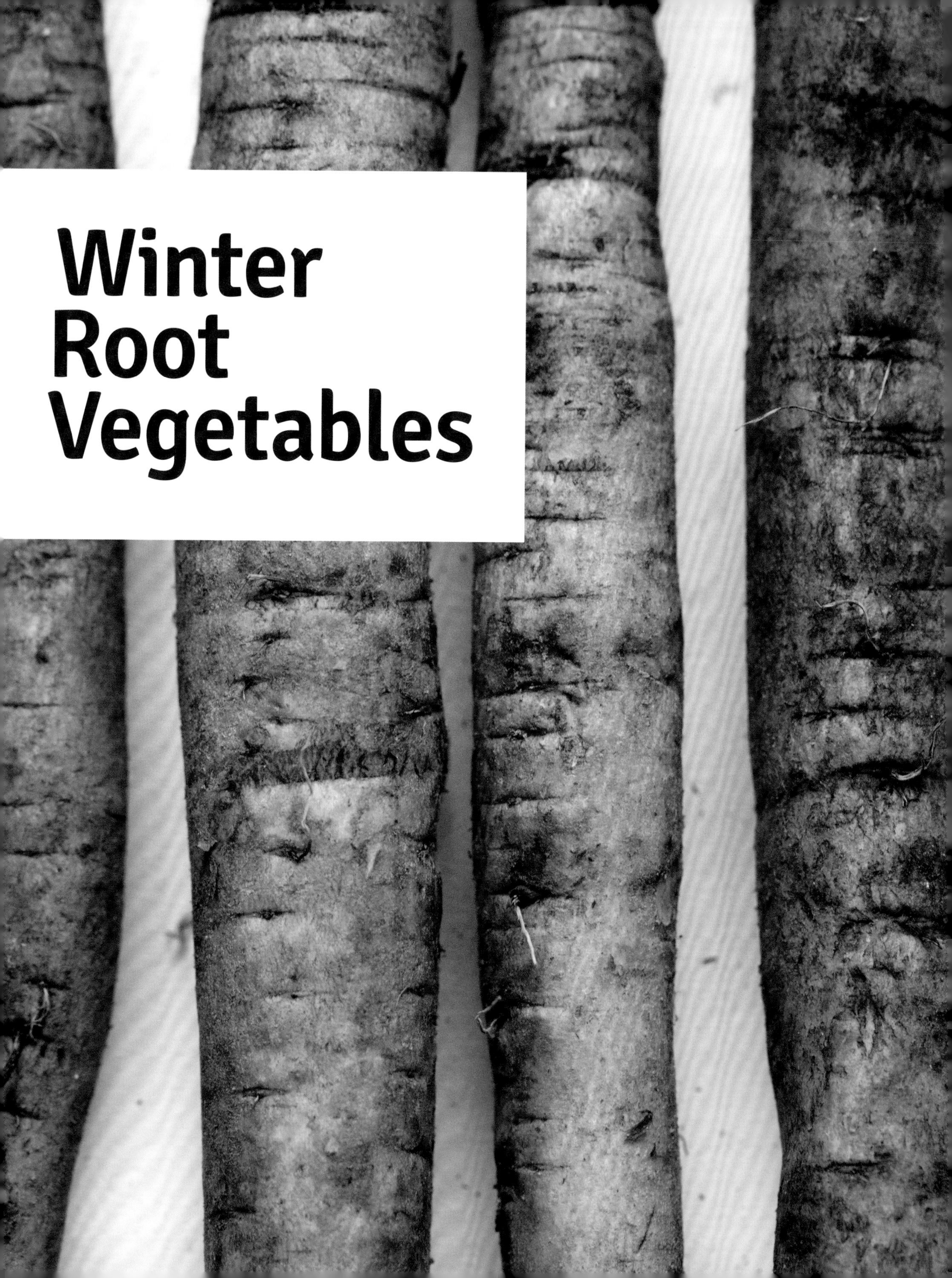

Winter Root Vegetables

FIELD GUIDE TO WINTER ROOT VEGETABLES

The following are some of our favorite heirloom and specialty varieties. The best place to find them is at your local farmers' market, or you can grow them yourself. The seeds are available through seed saver websites.

Atlas Carrot: An almost perfectly round, orange carrot. Named for its globe-like shape and the myth of the Titan who held up the spheres.

Burdock: Popular in Asia. Mildly sweet in flavor and deliciously pungent. Prized for its hearty texture.

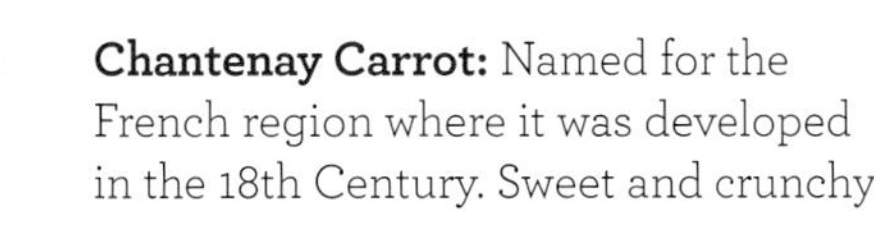

Chantenay Carrot: Named for the French region where it was developed in the 18th Century. Sweet and crunchy.

Cobalt Carrot: A dark, slightly mottled variety. Striking when sliced, with a crisp yellow core.

Dragon Carrot: A Chinese variety with a bright orange-yellow interior. Slightly spiced and nutty in flavor.

Deep Purple Carrot: Beautifully dark. Some are bluish-purple or nearly black. Color dissipates when cooked.

Nantes Carrot: An heirloom variety known for its near-cylindrical shape. Dates back to Netherlands cultivars grown in the 17th Century.

Ginger Root: Along with turmeric, a rhizome. When separated, any part of the plant may grow into an entirely new whole.

Hakurei Turnip: Snow-white and nearly perfect orbs. Mild and crispy. Delicious raw or lightly cooked. In Japanese cuisine, often pickled.

Horseradish: The secret ingredient in cocktail sauce. Clean, sharp flavor. Thrives in nearly all conditions.

Jicama: Also known as "Mexican yam" or "Mexican turnip." The edible root of a vine. Crisp pale interior, like that of a potato. Usually eaten raw in salads.

Parsnip: Similar to carrots, but sweeter, particularly after cooking. A staple of traditional British "Sunday roasts" and Christmas dinners.

Purple Top Turnip: One of the largest turnip varieties. Tender to the bite. Pale where it is planted underground and purple where it crowns above.

Rutabaga: A cross between the cabbage and the turnip. Leaves can be eaten as a vegetable. First described in print in 1620 by a Swiss botanist.

Sunchoke: A species of sunflower native to North America. Also called "Jerusalem artichoke." Its tuberous root is crisp and variant in color.

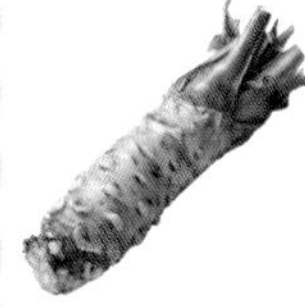

Wasabi: Also called "Japanese horseradish." Grated, its stem forms an extraordinarily powerful powder or paste.

ROOT VEGETABLES ARE a mainstay of winter cooking. From braises to roasts, from mashes to stews, these colorful tubers are among the heartiest vegetables available in any season. And it's no accident: they're packed with energy and nutrition precisely because of the cold weather.

Most root vegetables, like carrots, parsnips and turnips, are something called taproots. For all of you aspiring botanists out there, a taproot is the large, dominant root in a taproot system. It's the city center of the root metropolis; all of the other, smaller roots sprout out of it.

Taproots are thick and grow straight down. They store most of the plant's nutrients. Winter root vegetables are taproots that have saved up enough energy for an entire snowy season. When

we eat them, we're getting all of that dormant strength and nourishment. (Antioxidants supply their gorgeous, earthy hues, from yellow to orange to red to bluish-purple.)

But root vegetables aren't just amazing storage tanks; they're absolutely delicious-tasting, too. That's what residents of the Eastern Mediterranean discovered in the 10th Century CE. Before then, the carrot had been cultivated by the Romans, but never for its root. (The green top tastes faintly carroty, and it was used as an herb.) But suddenly the root burst onto the scene, and it has remained popular ever since. Long, bright and crunchy, it was originally eaten simply, with oil and vinegar. Now, it's beloved the world over, along with the rest of its root vegetable kin.

Braised Carrots, Mushrooms & Brussels Sprouts

with Creamy Polenta

In this dish, we're highlighting the natural sweetness of winter's carrots with oyster mushrooms. These delicious fungi are grown in temperate climates all over the world, and they have become a favorite of chefs and foragers alike. They usually appear on trees, in bountiful arrays, commonly without any stems. Their mild, earthy flavor and delicate texture make them a prized, gourmet mushroom among the many wild varieties available today.

MAKES 2 SERVINGS • ABOUT 515 CALORIES PER SERVING

Ingredients

6 Baby Carrots, Without Greens (About ½ Pound)
5 Ounces Oyster Mushrooms
3 Cloves Garlic
2 Sprigs Thyme
½ Pound Brussels Sprouts
¾ Cup Polenta
2 Tablespoons Butter
⅓ Cup Grated Parmesan Cheese
2 Tablespoons Tomato Paste
3 Tablespoons Vegetable Demi-Glace

1 Prepare the ingredients
Wash and dry the fresh produce. In a medium pot, heat 3 cups of salted water to boiling on high. Cut the carrots in half lengthwise, then in half crosswise on an angle. Roughly chop the oyster mushrooms. Peel and mince the garlic. Pick the thyme leaves off the woody stems; discard the stems and roughly chop the leaves. Remove and discard the roots and tough outer leaves of the Brussels sprouts; quarter the sprouts lengthwise.

2 Cook the polenta
Once the water is boiling, slowly stir in the polenta. Continue stirring to break up any lumps. Reduce the heat to low and simmer, stirring frequently, 10 to 12 minutes or until thickened. Remove from heat and stir in the butter and all but a pinch of the Parmesan cheese. Season with salt to taste and mix thoroughly to combine. Set aside in a warm place.

3 Start the vegetables
While the polenta cooks, in a large pan, heat 2 teaspoons of olive oil on medium-high until hot. Add the carrots, Brussels sprouts and oyster mushrooms; season with salt and pepper. Cook, stirring occasionally, 3 to 4 minutes, or until the vegetables begin to soften. Add the garlic and all but a pinch of the thyme; cook, stirring occasionally, 2 to 3 minutes, or until fragrant.

4 Add the tomato paste
Add the tomato paste to the pan of vegetables and cook, stirring frequently, 1 to 2 minutes, or until the tomato paste is brick red and caramelized.

5 Finish & plate your dish
Stir the vegetable demi-glace and 1 cup of water into the tomato-vegetable mixture, scraping up any browned bits from the bottom of the pan. Bring the mixture to a boil, then reduce the heat to low and simmer 3 to 5 minutes, or until thickened; season with salt and pepper to taste. To plate your dish, divide the cooked polenta between 2 plates. Top each with half the vegetables. Garnish with the remaining thyme and Parmesan cheese.

Chicken Sloppy Joe Sliders

with Kale Slaw & Homemade Pickles

These famous sandwiches, usually made with ground beef simmered in tomato sauce, may have originated in the 1900s at a bar in Old Havana, Cuba, called Sloppy Joe's. Since then, they've become a favorite throughout North America. Our version uses chicken instead of beef, for a lighter, healthier spin on the classic. We're also including a seasonal side: a kale slaw made with parsnips. Parsnips, which look like pale carrots, develop natural sugars in cool weather. Their raw, crisp sweetness is the perfect addition to this meal.

MAKES 2 SERVINGS • ABOUT 700 CALORIES PER SERVING

Ingredients

6 Potato Slider Buns
4 Cloves Garlic
1 Green Bell Pepper
1 Kirby Cucumber
1 Lemon
1 Medium Parsnip
1 Yellow Onion
½ Pound Green Kale
2 Tablespoons Champagne Vinegar
2 Tablespoons Mayonnaise
10 Ounces Ground Chicken
½ Cup Ketchup
2 Tablespoons Worcestershire Sauce
1 Tablespoon Light Brown Sugar

1 Prepare the ingredients

Wash and dry the fresh produce. Split open the slider buns. Peel all 4 garlic cloves. Smash 1 clove to flatten it. Mince the remaining cloves; using the flat side of your knife, smash until they resemble a paste. Cut out and discard the stem, ribs and seeds of the pepper; small dice the pepper. Cut the kirby cucumber into ⅛-inch-thick rounds and place in a heat-proof bowl or jar. Quarter the lemon and remove the seeds. Peel the parsnip, then cut into thick matchsticks. Peel and small dice the onion. Cut out and discard the kale stems; thinly slice the leaves into long strips.

2 Make the pickles

Add the Champagne vinegar to the cucumber slices. In a small pot, combine 1 cup of water, the smashed garlic clove and ½ teaspoon of salt. Heat to boiling on high. Once boiling, remove from heat and pour over the cucumber-vinegar mixture. Stir to thoroughly combine. Let stand while you continue cooking.

3 Dress the kale

In a small bowl, whisk together the mayonnaise, the juice of 3 lemon wedges and a pinch of the garlic paste; season with salt and pepper to taste. In a separate bowl, combine the kale, parsnip and some of the dressing (you may have extra dressing). Toss to coat and season with salt and pepper to taste.

4 Cook the aromatics & chicken

In a medium pan, heat 2 teaspoons of olive oil on medium-high until hot. Add the onion, green pepper and remaining garlic paste; season with salt and pepper. Cook, stirring occasionally, 4 to 5 minutes, or until softened. Add a little more olive oil and all of the ground chicken, then increase the heat to high. Cook, frequently breaking the chicken apart with a spoon, 5 to 6 minutes, or until cooked through. Season with salt and pepper.

5 Add the sauce & plate your dish

Once the chicken is cooked through, reduce the heat to medium and add the ketchup, Worcestershire sauce, light brown sugar and ¼ cup of water. Cook, stirring occasionally, 3 to 4 minutes, or until the sugar is completely dissolved and the sauce is slightly reduced in volume; season with salt and pepper to taste. Remove from heat and stir in the juice of the remaining lemon wedge. To plate your dish, divide the kale slaw between 2 plates. Fill each slider bun with the sloppy joe mixture and top with the pickles.

Flank Steak au Jus

with Roasted Dijon Cauliflower, Pickled Baby Turnips & Watercress

"Au jus" is a French culinary term for "with juice," and it usually refers to meat served with a pan sauce. When cooking steak, drippings and browned bits usually get left in the pan. But wait, there's flavor there! Deglazing these bits with demi-glace and simmering them with just a bit of water creates a rich sauce that enhances the dish. It's complete cooking, putting every bit of flavor right back into the finished steak. And to make it even better, you'll serve the steak with a side of pickled turnips. Pickling the turnips will partially cook them and give them a tart crunch to balance their natural sweetness.

MAKES 2 SERVINGS • ABOUT 640 CALORIES PER SERVING

Ingredients

10 Ounces Flank Steak
3 Cloves Garlic
3-4 Sprigs Tarragon
1 Lemon
½ Head Cauliflower (About 1 Pound)
½ Pound Baby Turnips, Without Greens
1 Tablespoon Granulated Sugar
2 Tablespoons Red Wine Vinegar
1 Tablespoon Smooth Dijon Mustard
3 Tablespoons Beef Demi-Glace
¼ Pound Watercress

1 Prepare the ingredients

Preheat the oven to 500°F. Wash and dry the fresh produce. Remove the steak from the refrigerator to bring to room temperature. Peel the garlic cloves. Smash 2 of the cloves. Mince the remaining clove; then, using the flat side of your knife, smash until it resembles a paste. Pick the tarragon leaves off the stems; discard the stems and finely chop the leaves. Quarter the lemon and remove the seeds. Remove and discard the core of the cauliflower; cut the head into small florets. Peel the turnip bulbs; halve the bulbs lengthwise.

2 Pickle the turnips

Place the turnips and red wine vinegar in a heatproof bowl or jar. In a small pot, combine the smashed garlic cloves, sugar, 1 cup of water, a little pepper and a big pinch of salt. Heat to boiling on high. Remove from heat and pour over the turnip-vinegar mixture. Set aside.

3 Roast & dress the cauliflower

Place the cauliflower on a sheet pan. Drizzle with olive oil and season with salt and pepper; toss to coat. Arrange in a single, even layer and roast, stirring halfway through, 14 to 16 minutes, or until browned. While the cauliflower roasts, in a small bowl, combine the tarragon, Dijon mustard and the juice of 2 lemon wedges. Slowly whisk in 2 teaspoons of olive oil; season with salt and pepper to taste. Once the cauliflower is finished, remove from the oven and cool for 2 minutes. Drizzle with the mustard mixture; toss to coat.

4 Cook the steak & make the jus

While the cauliflower roasts, pat the steak dry with paper towels and season with salt and pepper on both sides. In a large pan, heat 2 teaspoons of olive oil on medium until hot. Add the steak and cook, loosely covering the pan with aluminum foil, 3 to 4 minutes per side, or until it reaches your desired degree of doneness. Transfer the steak to a cutting board and let rest for at least 5 minutes. Carefully discard any oil from the pan, leaving the browned bits (or fond) in the pan. While the steak rests, add the beef demi-glace, ¼ cup of water and any accumulated juices from the resting steak to the pan of browned bits. Using a spoon or whisk, scrape up the fond from the bottom of the pan and simmer on medium-low, stirring occasionally, 1 to 3 minutes, or until slightly thickened.

5 Make the salad & plate your dish

In a large bowl, whisk together the garlic paste, the juice of the remaining lemon wedges and 2 teaspoons of olive oil. Add the watercress and as much of the pickled turnips as you'd like (draining before adding) and toss to coat; season with salt and pepper to taste. Find the lines of muscle (or grain) of the steak and thinly slice against the grain. Divide the sliced steak, cauliflower and salad between 2 plates. Top the steak with a spoonful of jus.

The Heart of the Flower: Bird's Foot Farm

EVEN WITH WINTER in the air, as the kaleidoscopic colors of the foliage turn and fall in the Adirondacks, there are still flowers that bloom. One native kind of sunflower unfurls its petals at Bird's Foot Farm in Canton, New York.

As the first frosts come across the valley, the flowers will fade; the leaves will curl back towards the soil. This process, called "dieback," is the plant readying itself for winter, diverting its energy. All the plant's nutrients go underground, forming the delicate tubers we eat—called sunchokes.

Winter is the best time to harvest them. And Bird's Foot Farm is an idyllic model of small farming. Harvesting is done by hand, by people who live on, and from, this land. It began as a collective during the back-to-the-land movement in 1972, one of thirteen such farms started in the area. As the movement waned, the region itself experienced something like dieback. Bird's Foot is the only farm of its kind to have survived.

However, the knowledge and practices championed by the movement have been preserved there through outreach and apprenticeship programs. Patreesha Endres, one of the farm's gardeners, says, "There's a new generation who are educating themselves. And it informs what they'll do, even if they don't become farmers."

Farms like Bird's Foot are dedicated to the ideals of seasonality. As America rediscovers and reinvigorates sustainable, seasonal cuisine and farming, we take one step closer to the land itself. As Patreesha says, "When you live with the seasons, they become a part of you."

Maple & Ginger Glazed Salmon

with Watercress, Orange & Parsnip Salad

Parsnips have been a staple food in Europe and Asia since ancient times. They resemble carrots in shape, but they have cream-colored, supple flesh. Though they can be harvested year-round, the best parsnips are plucked just after winter frosts. Cold weather turns some of the starch in parsnips to natural sugars and preserves their crunch, making them the perfect, subtly sweet addition to all kinds of dishes.

MAKES 2 SERVINGS • ABOUT 590 CALORIES PER SERVING

Ingredients

2 5-Ounce Skin-On Salmon Fillets
3 Scallions
2 Cloves Garlic
1 1-Inch Piece Ginger
1 Orange
1 Small Parsnip
1 Tablespoon Sunflower Seeds, Hulled & Raw
2 Tablespoons Maple Syrup
2 Tablespoons Soy Sauce
2 Teaspoons Sesame Oil
¼ Pound Watercress

1 Prepare the ingredients

Wash and dry the fresh produce. Remove the salmon from the refrigerator to bring to room temperature. Remove and discard the roots of the scallions; thinly slice the scallions on an angle, separating the white bottoms and green tops. Peel and thinly slice the garlic cloves. Peel and mince the ginger. Using a peeler, remove the rind of the orange, avoiding the white pith; mince the rind to get 2 teaspoons of zest. Halve the orange. Squeeze the juice of one half into a bowl. Cut off the pith and peel of the remaining orange half. Discard the pith and peel and cut the orange into bite-sized pieces. Place one-third of the white parts of the scallions into the bowl of orange juice. Peel and cut the parsnip into thin matchsticks.

2 Toast the sunflower seeds & make the vinaigrette

Heat a large pan (nonstick, if you have one) on medium-high until hot. Add the sunflower seeds and toast, stirring frequently, 2 to 3 minutes, or until lightly browned. Transfer to a small bowl and set aside. Wipe out the pan. To make the vinaigrette, season the orange juice-scallion mixture with salt and pepper. Slowly whisk in 2 tablespoons of olive oil until well combined.

3 Cook the salmon

Pat the salmon dry and season with salt and pepper on both sides. In the same pan used to toast the seeds, heat 2 teaspoons of oil on medium-high until hot. Add the fillets, skin-side down first, and cook, loosely covering the pan with aluminum foil, 3 to 5 minutes per side, or until the skin is crispy and the fish is cooked through. Transfer to a plate and cover with foil to keep warm. Wipe out the pan.

4 Glaze the salmon

In the same pan used to cook the fish, heat 2 teaspoons of oil on medium until hot. Add the garlic, ginger and remaining white parts of the scallions. Cook, stirring frequently, 30 seconds to 1 minute, or until softened and fragrant. Add the maple syrup, soy sauce, sesame oil and ¼ cup of water. Cook, stirring occasionally, 30 seconds to 1 minute, or until slightly thickened. Add the cooked salmon to the pan of glaze, skin-side down. Cook, spooning the sauce over the salmon, 1 to 2 minutes, or until the sauce is reduced in volume and thickened. Turn off the heat.

5 Finish & plate your dish

Just before serving, in a large bowl, combine the watercress, chopped orange, parsnip and toasted sunflower seeds; season with salt and pepper. Add in enough vinaigrette to coat the greens (you may have extra vinaigrette) and toss. To plate your dish, divide the glazed salmon and salad between 2 plates. Top each fillet with a spoonful of glaze. Garnish with the green parts of the scallions.

Winter Root Vegetable Stew

with Fresh Horseradish Gremolata

In this dish, you'll be using sunchokes, also called "Jerusalem artichokes." But they're not related to the artichoke at all! They're technically the roots of a particular kind of wispy sunflower native to Eastern North America. And though sunchoke flowers won't be winning any awards, the roots are exceptionally nutty and slightly sweet—the perfect winter vegetable for this hearty stew.

MAKES 2 SERVINGS • ABOUT 550 CALORIES PER SERVING

Ingredients

1 15-Ounce Can Cannellini Beans
4 Cloves Garlic
3-4 Sprigs Parsley
1 Medium Carrot
1 Yellow Onion
1 1-Inch Piece Fresh Horseradish
1 Lemon
1 Parsnip
½ Pound Sunchokes (About 5 or 6)
1 Mini Baguette
2 Fresh Bay Leaves
3 Tablespoons Vegetable Demi-Glace

1

2

3

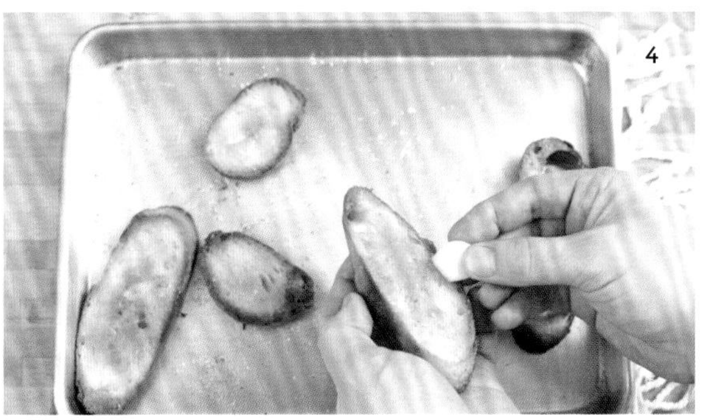

4

5

1 Prepare the ingredients

Preheat the oven to 425°F. Wash and dry the fresh produce. Drain and rinse the beans. Peel the garlic cloves. Leave 1 clove whole; mince the remaining cloves. Pick the parsley leaves off the stems; discard the stems and finely chop the leaves. Peel and small dice the carrot and onion. Peel and grate the horseradish. Using a peeler, remove the yellow rind of the lemon, avoiding the white pith; mince the rind to get 2 teaspoons of zest. Quarter the lemon and remove the seeds. Peel and medium dice the parsnip. Medium dice the sunchokes. Cut the bread on an angle into ¼-inch-thick slices.

2 Cook the aromatics

In a medium pot, heat 2 teaspoons of olive oil on medium-high until hot. Add the carrot, onion, parsnip and two-thirds of the minced garlic; season with salt and pepper. Cook, stirring frequently, 1 to 3 minutes, or until the onion starts to soften.

3 Add the vegetables

Add the sunchokes and season with salt and pepper. Cook, stirring occasionally, 2 to 3 minutes, or until the sunchokes have softened slightly. Add the beans, bay leaves, vegetable demi-glace and 2½ cups of water. Bring the mixture to a boil. Once boiling, reduce the heat to low and simmer, stirring occasionally, 16 to 20 minutes, or until the vegetables are tender and the stew has thickened slightly. Season with salt and pepper; remove from heat.

4 Toast the bread

While the stew simmers, drizzle the bread slices with olive oil. Place on a sheet pan and toast in the oven 4 to 6 minutes, or until browned and crispy. Remove from the oven. While still hot, rub with the whole garlic clove.

5 Make the horseradish gremolata

While the bread toasts, in a small bowl, combine the grated horseradish, lemon zest, chopped parsley and remaining minced garlic. Stir in enough olive oil to create a rough paste; season with salt and pepper to taste. Just before serving, stir the juice of 1 lemon wedge into the stew and the juice of 1 lemon wedge into the gremolata. To plate your dish, divide the stew between 2 bowls and garnish with the gremolata, garlic bread and remaining lemon wedges.

Sautéed Flounder

with Baby Root Vegetables & Brown Butter-Tamarind Sauce

In the world of root vegetables, smaller can often mean better. That's because the larger the plant, the less concentrated its flavor. Too small, and the vegetable is too hard or too young. But there's a happy medium. Baby turnips and fingerling potatoes achieve it. In this recipe, you'll pair them with seared flounder and tart tamarind for a dish that's as flavorful as it is tender.

MAKES 2 SERVINGS • ABOUT 600 CALORIES PER SERVING

Ingredients

¾ Pound Baby Turnips, Without Greens
½ Pound Fingerling Potatoes
1 Small Bunch Chives
1 Tablespoon Almonds, Raw & Whole
1 Tablespoon Pistachios, Shelled & Raw
2 6-Ounce Flounder Fillets
¼ Cup Rice Flour
1 Tablespoon Tamarind Concentrate
4 Tablespoons Butter

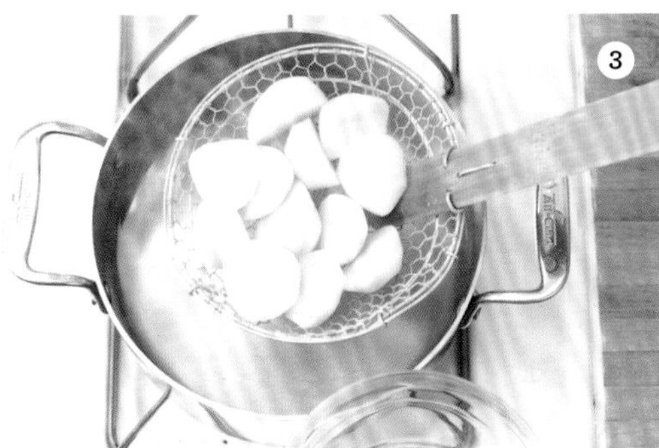

1 Prepare the ingredients

Preheat the oven to 425°F. Heat a large pot of salted water to boiling on high. Wash and dry the fresh produce. Peel and halve the baby turnips lengthwise. Halve the potatoes lengthwise. Cut the chives into 1-inch-long pieces. Roughly chop the almonds and pistachios.

2 Roast the potatoes

Toss the potatoes with 1 tablespoon of olive oil and season with salt and pepper. Place in a single layer on a sheet pan, cut-side down. Roast 12 to 14 minutes, or until browned and tender when pierced with a fork.

3 Cook the turnips

Once the water is boiling, add the turnips. Cook 4 to 6 minutes, or until tender when pierced with a fork. Drain thoroughly and set aside.

4 Toast the nuts & cook the flounder

While the vegetables cook, heat a medium, dry pan on medium-high. Add the almonds and pistachios and toast, stirring frequently, 2 to 3 minutes, or until fragrant and lightly browned. Transfer the nuts to a bowl and wipe out the pan. Pat the flounder fillets dry with a paper towel. Season with salt and pepper on both sides and coat with the rice flour (shaking off any excess). In a medium pan, heat 2 teaspoons of oil on high until hot. Add the coated fillets and cook 3 to 4 minutes per side, or until golden brown and cooked through. Transfer the cooked fillets to a paper towel-lined plate and season with salt. Wipe out the pan.

5 Make the brown butter-tamarind sauce

In a small bowl, combine the tamarind concentrate and ¼ cup of water. In the same pan used to cook the fish, melt the butter on medium heat and cook, stirring occasionally, 1 to 2 minutes, or until fragrant and deep golden brown. (The butter will bubble, then the foam will subside.) Stir in the diluted tamarind concentrate. (Be careful, as it may splatter.) Remove from heat and season with salt and pepper to taste. Add the cooked turnips; season with salt and pepper and toss to coat. To plate your dish, divide the fish, roasted potatoes and baby turnips between 2 plates. Top with a couple spoonfuls of the brown butter-tamarind sauce and garnish with the toasted almonds, pistachios and chives.

Potatoes

FIELD GUIDE TO POTATOES

The following are some of our favorite heirloom and specialty varieties. The best place to find them is at your local farmers' market, or you can grow them yourself. The seeds are available through seed saver websites.

Adirondack Blue: A stunning, hybrid variety with deep-blue skin and dark-purple flesh. First bred at Cornell University, and made available in 2003.

Gold Fingerling: Like all fingerlings, named for its faint resemblance to a finger. (A fingerling is a small, narrow variety.) Complex, versatile flavor.

Huckleberry: Pink interior with reddish, beet-like skin. Named for the wild huckleberry, native to the Northern Rockies.

Japanese Sweet Potato: Purplish or red skin. White or bright yellow underneath. Sweet and dry. Called "Satsumaimo" in Japanese.

Jewel Yam: Not actually a yam, but a sweet potato (incorrectly named because of its orange color). Starchy and delicious.

Kennebec: A prized culinary potato. Impressive taste. Fries well because of its low water content. Browns perfectly.

La Ratte: An heirloom fingerling. Popularized in France and Denmark. Hearty flavor. Buttery texture. Notes of chestnut.

Mountain Rose: Gorgeous, red-on-red variety. Small, tender and crisp. Named for the exquisite wildflower its interior resembles.

O'Henry Sweet Potato: A white-skinned heirloom variety. Dry in texture. As a result, a wonderful butter and flavor absorber.

Purple Passion: Named for its extraordinary, plum-like skin and royal-purple interior. Smooth texture. Sweet in flavor.

Rose Finn Apple: A slender fingerling with rosy skin and crispy flesh. Best prepared simply because of its natural taste.

Ruby Fingerling: A large, curved fingerling, prized for its delicious flesh. Firm, crisp and waxy. Red skin, with yellow interior.

Ruby Sensation: Red on the outside, creamy on the inside. A small potato with big, nutty taste. Moist, waxy texture. Good for boiling.

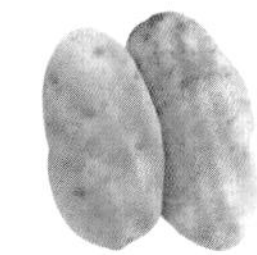

Russet: A large variety. Dry, white flesh. Bakes well. Great for fluffy, creamy mashed potatoes. Largely grown in Idaho.

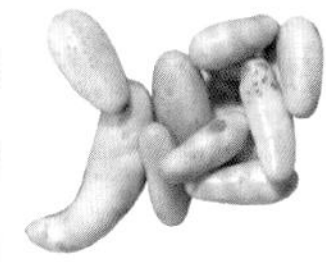

Russian Banana: Often confused with premature "new" potatoes, but actually small when fully grown. Mild and nutty.

White Delight: A pale, floury potato. Great for mashing, baking and French fries (unlike waxy varieties, which tend to be better boiled).

White Sweet Potato: Similar to orange sweet potato varieties, but with a milder flavor. Used in both sweet and savory dishes.

Yukon Gold: Smooth skin, free of divots (or "eyes"). First developed in the 1960s at the University of Guelph in Ontario, Canada.

LIKE CORN, BEANS and squash, potatoes are indigenous to the Americas. Originally grown at high altitudes in the modern-day South American region encompassing Bolivia and Peru, potatoes have been cooked for over 2,000 years. Then and now, they're almost unbelievably hardy: some can essentially grow in snow, while others can thrive at 13,000-foot elevations.

After explorers brought the potato to Europe, it gradually emerged as a global staple—most notably in Ireland. There, it became so essential that tragedy ensued when the crop withered with disease, resulting in a famine. At first, however, Northern Protestants refused to grow the plant, since it wasn't mentioned in the Bible. (A minister overcame this hurdle by planting the seeds on

Good Friday, then sprinkling them with holy water.)

In France, the potato was also rejected by the common people—until a daring nobleman successfully popularized it, fulfilling a lifelong dream. (The man had spent time in a German prison where potatoes were served, and, bizarrely, he grew to love them passionately.) Paying guards to stand by his potato fields at night, he convinced locals that the plant was highly valuable. He even convinced the queen, Marie Antoinette, to don a white crown of potato flowers.

Unlike the *Ancien Régime*, potatoes have survived. They vary beautifully and deliciously in appearance and texture. Use waxy potatoes for boiling, floury potatoes for mashing and sweet potatoes for just about everything "winter."

Mushroom Steam Buns

with Miso Butter & Japanese Purple Sweet Potato Salad

You'll never think of potato salad the same way again. This version uses Okinawan sweet potatoes, a hearty variety with white skin and a brilliantly purple core. In addition to being absolutely gorgeous, these potatoes are rich in flavor and slightly sweet, and they contain more antioxidants than a handful of blueberries. We can't wait for you to cut one open!

MAKES 2 SERVINGS • ABOUT 580 CALORIES PER SERVING

Ingredients

2 Scallions
2 Sprigs Thai Basil
1 Lime
1 Pound Okinawan Sweet Potatoes
½ Pound King Trumpet Mushrooms
2 Teaspoons Cornstarch
2 Tablespoons Soy Sauce
1 Tablespoon Butter
1 Tablespoon White Miso Paste
2 Teaspoons Sesame Oil
2 Tablespoons Mayonnaise
1 Tablespoon Rice Vinegar, Unseasoned
6 Chinese Steam Buns

1 Prepare the ingredients

Wash and dry the fresh produce. Heat a medium pot of water to boiling on high. Remove and discard the roots of the scallions; thinly slice the scallions, separating the white bottoms and green tops. Pick the Thai basil leaves off the stems; discard the stems. Using a peeler, remove the green rind of the lime, avoiding the white pith; mince the rind to get 2 teaspoons of zest. Quarter the lime. Peel the potatoes and cut into bite-sized pieces. Small dice the mushrooms.

2 Cook the potatoes

Once the pot of water is boiling, add the potatoes. Cook 18 to 22 minutes, or until tender when pierced with a fork. Drain thoroughly and transfer to a bowl. Place the potatoes in the refrigerator to cool as you continue cooking. Rinse out the pot and fill with 1 inch of water. Return the pot to the stove and heat to boiling on medium-high.

3 Make the mushroom sauce & miso butter

While the potatoes cook, make the mushroom sauce in a small bowl by combining the cornstarch, soy sauce and ¼ cup of water. To make the miso butter, in a small pot, heat the butter, miso paste, lime zest and 2 tablespoons of water on low. Cook, whisking constantly, 2 to 3 minutes, or until the butter is melted and the mixture is thoroughly combined. Remove from heat and set aside in a warm place.

4 Cook the mushrooms & dress the potatoes

In a large pan, heat 2 teaspoons of olive oil on medium until hot. Add the mushrooms and cook, stirring occasionally, 3 to 5 minutes, or until slightly browned and cooked through. Reduce the heat to low and add the mushroom sauce and white parts of the scallions. Cook, stirring occasionally, 30 seconds to 1 minute, or until thickened. Remove from heat and set aside. Remove the cooked potatoes from the refrigerator and stir in the sesame oil, mayonnaise, rice vinegar, green parts of the scallions and the juice of 2 lime wedges. Stir until well combined and season with salt and pepper to taste. Let stand at room temperature.

5 Steam the buns & plate your dish

Place a colander on top of the pot of boiling water, making sure that the water isn't high enough to touch the colander. Place the steam buns into the colander and tightly cover with the lid of the pot. Steam 3 to 4 minutes, or until the buns are softened and puffy. Using tongs, transfer the steamed buns to a plate and fill each with the mushroom filling. To plate your dish, divide the assembled buns and potato salad between 2 plates. Garnish with the Thai basil leaves. Serve with the miso butter on the side for dipping.

Provençal Fish Stew

with Toasted Baguette & Aioli

The original, petite, elongated fingerling potato is native to South America. During the Colonial period, it was brought to Europe, where its superior flavor and interesting shape made it a standard, especially in French cuisine. In one of cooking's folksier stories, an American businessman was traveling in France to buy a racehorse when he was served these delicious little potatoes. When he asked for a few to bring back stateside, he was summarily dismissed by the chef. However, when he returned home (horse in tow) he noticed something strange in the animal's feedbag. It was an heirloom fingerling! He planted it immediately, completing the variety's tri-continental journey.

MAKES 2 SERVINGS • ABOUT 600 CALORIES PER SERVING

Ingredients

6 Ounces Multicolored Fingerling Potatoes
4 Cloves Garlic
3 Tablespoons Kalamata Olives, With Pits
3-4 Sprigs Parsley
1 Lemon
1 Small Red Onion
1 Mini Baguette
1 6-Ounce Salmon Fillet
1 6-Ounce Cod Fillet
1 15-Ounce Can Diced Tomatoes
¼ Cup Mayonnaise

1 Prepare the ingredients

Preheat the oven to 375°F. Wash and dry the fresh produce. Heat a medium pot of salted water to boiling on high. Thinly slice the potatoes into ¼-inch-thick rounds. Peel the garlic cloves. Thinly slice 3 of the cloves. Mince the remaining clove; using the side of your knife, smash until it resembles a paste. Using the side of your knife, flatten the olives to remove and discard the pits. Roughly chop the olives. Pick the parsley leaves off the stems; discard the stems. Roughly chop the parsley. Quarter the lemon and remove the seeds. Peel and small dice the onion.

2 Toast the baguette

Cut the baguette on an angle into ¼-inch-thick slices and place on a sheet pan. Drizzle the baguette with olive oil and season with salt and pepper. Bake 8 to 10 minutes, or until golden brown.

3 Cook the potatoes

While the baguette toasts, add the potatoes to the pot of boiling water. Cook 8 to 10 minutes, or until tender when pierced with a fork. Drain thoroughly and wipe out the pot.

4 Make the stew

Cut each fish fillet into large pieces, then season with salt and pepper on all sides. In the pot used for the potatoes, heat 2 teaspoons of olive oil on medium until hot. Add the garlic and onion; season with salt and pepper. Cook, stirring occasionally, 3 to 4 minutes, or until the onions are translucent. Stir in the diced tomatoes and simmer for 2 to 3 minutes. Stir in the cooked potatoes, seasoned fish pieces and half of both the parsley and olives. Cook, stirring occasionally, 4 to 6 minutes, or until the fish is opaque and cooked through. (Be sure to stir carefully so that the fish pieces don't break apart.) Season with salt and pepper to taste.

5 Make the aioli & plate your dish

While the stew simmers, in a small bowl, combine the mayonnaise, garlic paste and the juice of 2 lemon wedges; season with salt and pepper to taste and stir until well combined. When the stew is finished, divide between 2 bowls and sprinkle with the remaining chopped olives. Lay the toasted baguette slices over the top of the stew and spoon the aioli on top. Garnish with the remaining parsley and lemon wedges.

Warm Winter Sweet Potato Salad

with Beluga Lentils & Apple Cider Vinaigrette

Sweet potatoes, despite their name, are only very distant relatives of the potato. Technically, sweet potatoes belong to a different family and aren't nightshades. They're close kin to morning glories (the beautiful, trumpeting flowers). Sweet potatoes don't have their signature, sugary flavor when raw. Heat transforms the natural starches, breaking them down into sugars. So, you'll cook them before adding them to the salad. Their brightness is complemented by earthy, nutty lentils and a zesty apple cider vinaigrette.

MAKES 2 SERVINGS • ABOUT 700 CALORIES PER SERVING

Ingredients

1½ Pounds Sweet Potato
2 Stalks Celery
1 Clove Garlic
1 Small Red Onion
¼ Cup Walnuts, Shelled & Raw
½ Cup Beluga Lentils
2 Tablespoons Apple Cider Vinegar
1 Tablespoon Honey
2 Teaspoons Dijon Mustard
2 Tablespoons Dried Currants
1 Bunch Microgreens

1

2

3

4

5

1 Prepare the ingredients
Wash and dry the fresh produce. Heat a medium pot of salted water to boiling on high. Peel the sweet potatoes and cut into thin rounds, then matchsticks. Thinly slice the celery on an angle. Peel and mince the garlic; using the flat side of your knife, smash until it resembles a paste. Peel and thinly slice the onion. Roughly chop the walnuts.

2 Cook the sweet potatoes
Add the sweet potato matchsticks to the boiling water. Cook 3 to 5 minutes, or until tender, but still slightly firm. Using a slotted spoon or tongs, transfer the cooked sweet potato to a bowl, leaving the water boiling in the pot.

3 Cook the lentils
To the same pot of boiling water used to cook the sweet potatoes, add the lentils. Cook 15 to 20 minutes, or until tender. Drain thoroughly and set aside.

4 Toast the walnuts
While the lentils cook, heat a small, dry pan on medium-high until hot. Add the chopped walnuts and toast, stirring frequently, 2 to 3 minutes, or until browned and nuttily fragrant. Transfer to a small bowl.

5 Dress the salad & plate your dish
In a small bowl, combine the garlic paste, vinegar, honey and Dijon mustard; season with salt and pepper to taste. Slowly whisk in 2 tablespoons of olive oil until well combined. In a large bowl, combine the cooked sweet potatoes, celery, onion, toasted walnuts, lentils and currants. Add in enough of the vinaigrette to coat the salad (you may have extra vinaigrette); gently toss to mix. Divide the salad between 2 plates; garnish with the microgreens.

Pan-Seared Chicken Quarters

with Purple Smashed Potatoes, Brussels Sprouts & Warm Bacon Vinaigrette

In this recipe, you'll be using purple potatoes to add beauty and a subtle, earthy flavor to your meal. Purple (sometimes called blue) potatoes are native to the Americas and were among the first varieties to be cultivated by indigenous peoples in the area of Lake Titicaca. These potatoes get their vivid hue from a concentration of antioxidants, the same healthy nutrients that color blueberries and pomegranates.

MAKES 2 SERVINGS • ABOUT 600 CALORIES PER SERVING

Ingredients

3-4 Sprigs Parsley
1 Small Bunch Chives
1 Clove Garlic
1 Shallot
½ Pound Purple Potatoes
½ Pound Brussels Sprouts
2 Slices Bacon
2 Chicken Leg Quarters (About 9-10 Ounces Each)
1 Tablespoon White Wine Vinegar

1 Prepare the ingredients

Wash and dry the fresh produce. Heat a medium pot of salted water to boiling on high. Pick the parsley leaves off the stems; discard the stems and roughly chop the leaves. Finely chop the chives. Peel and mince the garlic; using the flat side of your knife, smash until it resembles a paste. Peel and thinly slice the shallot. Cut the potatoes into bite-sized pieces. Trim off and discard the ends of the Brussels sprouts; halve each lengthwise. Cut the bacon into small pieces.

2 Cook the potatoes

Once the water is boiling, add the potatoes. Cook 12 to 14 minutes, or until very tender when pierced with a fork. Drain thoroughly and return to the pot. Add the garlic paste, all but a pinch of the chives, half the parsley and 1 tablespoon of olive oil. Using a fork, smash the potatoes until smooth. Stir to incorporate and season with salt and pepper to taste.

3 Cook the bacon

While the potatoes cook, heat a medium pan on medium-high until hot. Add the bacon and cook, stirring occasionally, 4 to 5 minutes, or until crispy. Transfer to a paper towel-lined plate, leaving any fat in the pan.

4 Cook the chicken & Brussels sprouts

Season the chicken with salt and pepper on both sides. In the same pan used to cook the bacon, heat the leftover bacon fat on medium until hot. Add the chicken and cook, loosely covering the pan with aluminum foil, 5 to 6 minutes on the first side, or until browned. Turn over the chicken and add the Brussels sprouts, replacing the foil cover; cook, without stirring, 2 to 4 minutes. Flip the Brussels sprouts and cook 3 to 5 minutes longer, or until the chicken is cooked through and the Brussels sprouts are browned. Transfer both to a plate, leaving any drippings (or fond) in the pan.

5 Make the bacon vinaigrette & plate your dish

Heat the reserved fond in the pan on medium until hot. Add the shallot and cook, stirring frequently, 45 seconds to 1 minute, or until softened. Add the white wine vinegar and ¼ cup of water, scraping up any browned bits from the bottom of the pan. Cook, stirring occasionally, 2 to 3 minutes, or until slightly reduced in volume. Stir in the cooked bacon and remaining parsley. Remove from heat; season with salt and pepper to taste. To plate your dish, divide the potatoes and Brussels sprouts between 2 plates. Lay the chicken over the top; spoon the bacon vinaigrette over the chicken. Garnish with the remaining chives.

Creamy Sweet Potato & Kale Casserole

with Berbere Spice & Ginger

Sweet potatoes aren't just delicious—they're beautiful and good for you. They get their orange color from beta-carotenes, the same pigment found in carrots and pumpkins. In this dish, they're a hearty pop of flavor in a classic casserole. To spice it up, we're using Berbere, a rich blend commonly found in Ethiopian and Eritrean cuisines. The warmth of these spices provides the perfect accent for the hearty winter ingredients of this meal.

MAKES 2 SERVINGS • ABOUT 645 CALORIES PER SERVING

Ingredients

¾ Pound Sweet Potatoes
1 Bunch Curly Kale
3 Tablespoons Pecans, Raw & Unshelled
1 1-Inch Piece Ginger
5 Ounces Egg Noodles
2 Tablespoons Butter
2 Tablespoons All-Purpose Flour
½ Teaspoon Berbere Spice Blend
1 Cup Low-Fat Milk
⅓ Cup Grated Parmesan Cheese
¼ Cup Panko Breadcrumbs

1 Prepare the ingredients
Preheat the oven to 475°F. Wash and dry the fresh produce. Heat 2 large pots of salted water to boiling on high. Peel and medium dice the sweet potatoes. Remove and discard the kale stems; roughly chop the leaves. Roughly chop the pecans. Peel and mince the ginger.

2 Cook the sweet potatoes
Once the first pot of water is boiling, add the sweet potatoes. Cook 7 to 9 minutes, or until tender when pierced with a fork. Drain thoroughly; transfer to a large bowl.

3 Cook the noodles
Once the second pot of water is boiling, add the egg noodles. Cook 5 to 6 minutes, or until just shy of al dente. Drain thoroughly and transfer to the bowl of cooked sweet potatoes. Set aside. Rinse and dry the pot.

4 Make the filling
In the same pot used to cook the pasta, melt the butter on medium-high heat. Add the minced ginger; cook, stirring frequently, 1 to 2 minutes, or until fragrant and slightly softened. Add the flour and Berbere spice blend; cook, stirring frequently, 30 seconds to 1 minute, or until toasted and fragrant. Slowly add the milk and ¾ cup of water and cook, stirring occasionally, 3 to 4 minutes, or until thickened. Season with salt and pepper. Stir in the kale and Parmesan cheese; cook, stirring frequently, 1 to 2 minutes, or until the kale has wilted. Add the cooked sweet potatoes and noodles; stir until thoroughly combined and season with salt and pepper to taste.

5 Bake & serve your dish
Transfer the mixture to an oven-safe baking dish. Sprinkle with the panko breadcrumbs and pecans. Bake 14 to 16 minutes, or until browned and bubbly. Let stand for at least 2 minutes before serving.

Nuts

FIELD GUIDE TO NUTS

The following are some of our favorite varieties from around the world. If you can't find them in your local grocery store, check out the nearest spice shop or specialty foods store.

Acorn: The nut of the oak tree and its relatives. Consumed by humans since pre-history. Hardiness makes them perfect for storing.

Almond: Native to the Middle East and South Asia. A member of the rose family along with peaches and nectarines.

Beech Nut: Native to temperate forests of North America, Europe and Asia. Spiny shells contain small, intensely woody morsels.

Brazil Nut: Grown on a tree native to South America. The fruit takes 14 months to mature, weighs four pounds and contains 8 to 24 edible seeds (nuts).

Cashew: Grown on a species of tropical evergreen tree. Unlike most nuts, cashews contain starch, making them ideal for thickening stews.

Chestnut: Closely related to the beech and oak. At one time, chestnut trees made up one-quarter of Appalachian forests.

Coconut: Like almonds and pistachios, not technically a nut. These are "drupes," or hard seed shells that form inside of fruits.

Ginkgo Nut: A traditional Asian nut found in congee (a traditional rice porridge). Fresh ginkgo pods have a ripe, almost cheese-like odor.

Hazelnut: Also called filberts or cobnuts, they have been cultivated in Europe for 9,000 years.

Kola Nut: The seeds of a tree native to tropical African rainforests. Contains caffeine. Used to flavor and caffeinate beverages.

Macadamia Nut: Native to Australia. The first commercial orchards were planted there in the 1880s. Planted extensively in Hawaii in the 1920s.

Peanut: First domesticated and farmed in Paraguay. Spread north to Mexico and the U.S. Technically a legume (like beans and lentils).

Pecan: In the hickory family. The word pecan comes from an Algonquin word that means "nut that requires a stone to crack."

Pine Nut: Found between the scales of pine cones. About 20 large varieties have culinary uses. Have been a part of human diets for tens of thousands of years.

Pistachio: A member of the cashew family, originally from the Middle East and Central Asia. In the Hanging Gardens of Babylon.

Walnut: Early Romans considered them food for gods. Brought to California in the 1700s, where they continue to thrive.

TECHNICALLY SPEAKING, A nut is a dried tree fruit with a hard shell around a seed. But as we typically use the term, other types of plants are included. A peanut, for instance, is not a nut, strictly speaking. It's a legume, like a pea or a bean. The same applies to other "nuts," like pecans and pistachios.

However, even using a broad definition, nuts share certain characteristics. First, they're highly concentrated. Their low water content means that, in very little space, they pack an astonishing amount of nutrition. This includes high protein content and an abundance of healthy fats (particulary in walnuts and almonds). Second, because of their shells, they're extraordinarily durable. Naturally perfect

containers, their shells keep them whole, dry and delicious through the winter.

These characteristics have made nuts a part of human diets for millennia. In Italy, the original recipe for polenta featured chestnut meal. (This was back before maize was introduced to Europe from the Americas.) Tools for breaking nut shells date back 780,000 years. Fossil records show that certain varieties of acorn-bearing oak trees were growing on Pangaea, before the continents split. Some of those varieties are still used for food.

Today, nuts are highly valued, not just for their sustenance, but for their texture and taste. Even in small quantities, they add exquisite flavor to milder dishes and unmatched, crispy crunch to garnishes and sautés.

Baked Acorn Squash

with Chestnut, Leek & Apple Stuffing

Chestnuts are popular around the holidays because they're harvested in the colder months. Chestnut trees grow throughout Asia, Europe and the U.S., making the nuts a prized ingredient for both sweet and savory dishes in many different cuisines. In this recipe, you'll use chestnuts that are already roasted and peeled to reveal the starchy nut's subtle sweetness. With sautéed leek and apple, this robust stuffing served in baked acorn squash is so impressive, it could double as a centerpiece.

MAKES 2 SERVINGS • ABOUT 625 CALORIES PER SERVING

Ingredients

2 Sprigs Thyme
3-4 Sprigs Parsley
2 Cloves Garlic
1 Acorn Squash (About 1½ Pounds)
1 Fuji Apple
1 Stalk Celery
1 Medium Leek
½ Rye Bread Boule (About ½ Pound)
⅓ Cup Chestnuts, Peeled & Roasted
2 Tablespoons Butter
1 Cup Vegetable Broth

1 Prepare the ingredients
Preheat the oven to 425°F. Wash and dry the fresh produce. Pick the thyme and parsley leaves off the stems; discard the stems and roughly chop the leaves. Peel and mince the garlic. Cut the acorn squash in half and scoop out the seeds. Peel, core and medium dice the apple. Small dice the celery. Cut the leek lengthwise and rinse thoroughly to remove any dirt between the layers; small dice the leek. Cut the rye bread boule into 1-inch cubes. Roughly chop the chestnuts.

2 Roast the squash
Drizzle the insides of the acorn squash with olive oil and season with salt and pepper. Roast on a sheet pan, skin-side down, 18 to 21 minutes, or until the flesh is tender when pierced with a knife.

3 Toast the bread
While the squash roasts, place the bread cubes on a separate sheet pan. Bake 8 to 10 minutes, or until browned and crispy.

4 Make the stuffing
In a large pan, melt the butter with 2 teaspoons of olive oil on medium-high. Once melted, add the garlic, leek and celery; season with salt and pepper. Cook, stirring frequently, 2 to 3 minutes, or until the vegetables have softened. Add the toasted bread cubes, chestnuts, apple, thyme and all but a pinch of the parsley (reserve the rest for garnish). Stir in the vegetable broth and season with salt and pepper. Cook, stirring frequently, 2 to 3 minutes, or until the broth is absorbed. Season with salt and pepper to taste and remove from heat.

5 Stuff the squash & plate your dish
Fill the roasted squash halves with as much stuffing as possible. Return the squash to the sheet pan. Place any leftover stuffing around the base of the squash to stabilize them while they roast. Cover tightly with aluminum foil and roast 8 to 10 minutes. Remove the foil and roast another 6 to 8 minutes, or until browned. To plate your dish, place 1 stuffed squash half on each plate, then divide the remaining stuffing between the plates. Garnish with the remaining parsley.

Pan-Roasted Chicken Quarters

with Dried Cherry & Pistachio Quinoa

The green pistachios we recognize today have been eaten for at least 8,000 years. The pistachio tree was even cultivated in the Hanging Gardens of Babylon (one of the Seven Wonders of the World). The earliest evidence of the Atlantic pistachio, a close relative, dates back almost 780,000 years! We're joining in the longstanding tradition and serving them up with dried cherries, white quinoa and succulent chicken quarters.

MAKES 2 SERVINGS • ABOUT 655 CALORIES PER SERVING

Ingredients

2 Chicken Leg Quarters (About 9-10 Ounces Each)
3 Tablespoons Dried Cherries
3 Tablespoons Pistachios, Shelled & Raw
3-4 Sprigs Parsley
2 Cloves Garlic
1 Shallot
½ Cup White Quinoa
5 Ounces Baby Spinach
½ Cup Crumbled Feta Cheese

1

2

3

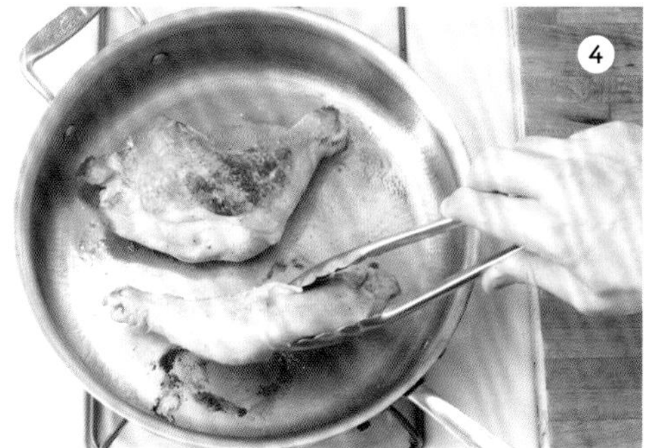
4

5

1 Prepare the ingredients

Wash and dry the fresh produce. Heat a medium pot of salted water to boiling on high. Remove the chicken quarters from the refrigerator to bring to room temperature. Roughly chop the cherries and pistachios. Pick the parsley leaves off the stems; discard the stems and roughly chop the leaves. Peel and mince the garlic and shallot.

2 Cook the quinoa

Once the water is boiling, add the quinoa. Cook 11 to 13 minutes, or until tender. Drain thoroughly and set aside.

3 Toast the pistachios

While the quinoa cooks, heat a large, dry pan on medium until hot. Add the pistachios and toast, stirring frequently, 3 to 5 minutes, or until browned and fragrant. Transfer to a small bowl and wipe out the pan.

4 Cook the chicken

While the quinoa continues to cook, season the chicken with salt and pepper on both sides. In the same pan used to toast the nuts, heat 2 teaspoons of olive oil on medium until hot. Add the seasoned chicken, skin-side down. Cook, loosely covering the pan with aluminum foil, 13 to 15 minutes per side, or until the skin is browned and the chicken is cooked through (the juices should run clear). Transfer the chicken to a plate, leaving any drippings (or fond) in the pan. Loosely cover the plate with aluminum foil to keep warm and set aside.

5 Make the quinoa salad & plate your dish

To the pan of reserved fond, add 1 teaspoon of olive oil and heat on medium until hot. Add the shallot and garlic; season with salt and pepper. Cook, stirring frequently, 30 to 45 seconds, or until fragrant. Add the spinach; season with salt and pepper. Cook, stirring frequently, 1 to 2 minutes, or until wilted. Stir in the chopped cherries, toasted pistachios, cooked quinoa and half the parsley. Cook, stirring occasionally, 1 to 2 minutes, or until thoroughly combined and heated through. Remove from heat and season with salt and pepper to taste. To plate your dish, divide the quinoa salad between 2 plates and top each with a chicken quarter. Garnish with the feta cheese and remaining parsley.

Pan-Seared Salmon

with Candied Orange Peel & Cranberry-Walnut Stuffing

The savory stuffing you'll create here as a side dish for seared salmon is dotted with jewel-like cranberries and crunchy walnuts. The burst of bright citrus flavor comes from fresh-squeezed orange juice. We also candied the orange peel by coating it in sugar and caramelizing it in the oven, to create an intensely bittersweet flavor perfect for both the salmon and the stuffing.

MAKES 2 SERVINGS • ABOUT 530 CALORIES PER SERVING

Ingredients

2 6-Ounce Salmon Fillets
1 Mini Baguette
2 Cloves Garlic
3-4 Sprigs Parsley
2 Sprigs Sage
2 Sprigs Thyme
1 Medium Parsnip
1 Yellow Onion
1 Stalk Celery
1 Orange
¼ Cup Walnuts, Shelled & Raw
1 Tablespoon Granulated Sugar
¼ Cup Dried Cranberries
1 Cup Vegetable Broth

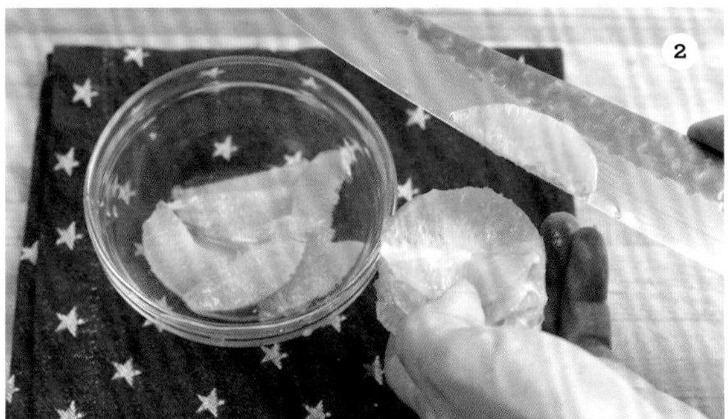

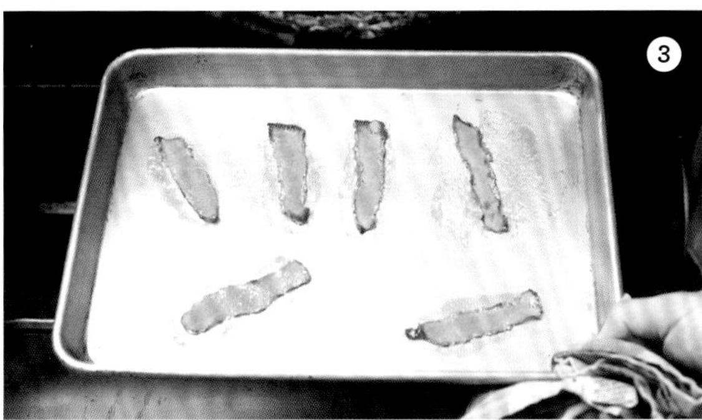

1 Prepare the ingredients

Preheat the oven to 400°F. Wash and dry the fresh produce. Remove the salmon from the refrigerator to bring to room temperature. Cut the baguette into ½-inch cubes. Peel and mince the garlic. Pick the parsley, sage and thyme leaves off the stems; discard the stems and roughly chop the sage, thyme and all but a few parsley leaves. Peel the parsnip and onion. Small dice the parsnip, onion and celery. Using a peeler, remove the orange rind, avoiding the white pith. Roughly chop the walnuts.

2 Toast the bread & make the orange supremes

Arrange the baguette cubes on a sheet pan in an even layer. Bake 5 to 6 minutes, or until browned. Transfer to a large bowl and wipe off the sheet pan. While the bread bakes, using a knife, cut away and discard any remaining white pith from the orange. Carefully cut out the segments (or supremes) from between the membranes and place in a small bowl. Squeeze the juice from the leftover membranes into a separate small bowl; discard the membranes. To the bowl of supremes, add half the thyme and about 1 teaspoon of olive oil; season with salt and pepper to taste.

3 Candy the orange peel

Thoroughly coat the orange peel in the sugar and place on the same sheet pan used to toast the bread. Bake 3 to 5 minutes, or until slightly browned. Remove from the oven and immediately flip to prevent sticking.

4 Make the stuffing

In a large pan (nonstick, if you have one), heat 2 teaspoons of olive oil on medium-high until hot. Add the garlic, parsnip, onion and celery; season with salt and pepper. Cook, stirring occasionally, 2 to 3 minutes, or until softened. Stir in the sage, chopped parsley and remaining thyme; cook, stirring occasionally, 1 to 2 minutes, or until well combined and heated through. Stir in the toasted bread cubes, walnuts, cranberries, reserved orange juice and vegetable broth; season with salt and pepper to taste. Remove from heat and transfer the stuffing to a 2-quart baking dish. Cover tightly with foil and bake 8 to 10 minutes. Remove the foil and bake 8 to 10 minutes longer, or until browned and crisped on the top.

5 Cook the salmon & plate your dish

While the stuffing bakes, season the salmon with salt and pepper on both sides. In the same pan used to make the stuffing, heat 2 teaspoons of olive oil on medium until hot. Add the salmon, skinless-side down; cook 3 to 5 minutes, or until browned. Flip the fillets and cook 5 to 7 minutes, or until cooked through. Place a fillet on each plate and garnish each with the candied orange peel. Divide the orange supremes and stuffing between the plates. Garnish with the whole parsley leaves.

Macadamia-Crusted Cod

with Forbidden Rice Salad, Golden Beets & Avocado

Macadamia trees, though we may associate them most closely with Hawaii, are actually Australian natives. The trees have been cultivated since the 1800s and have spread to temperate climates across the world. Macadamia trees take 7 to 10 years to mature, but once mature, they can produce for up to 100 years. The nut itself is uniquely flavored and buttery. In this recipe, we're using it to create a toasty, delicious crust for tender cod.

MAKES 2 SERVINGS • ABOUT 700 CALORIES PER SERVING

Ingredients

¾ Cup Forbidden Rice
½ Pound Baby Golden Beets, Without Greens
3-4 Sprigs Mint
3 Scallions
1 Lime
1 Avocado
¼ Cup Macadamia Nuts, Roasted & Unsalted
2 Tablespoons Panko Breadcrumbs
2 5-Ounce Cod Fillets

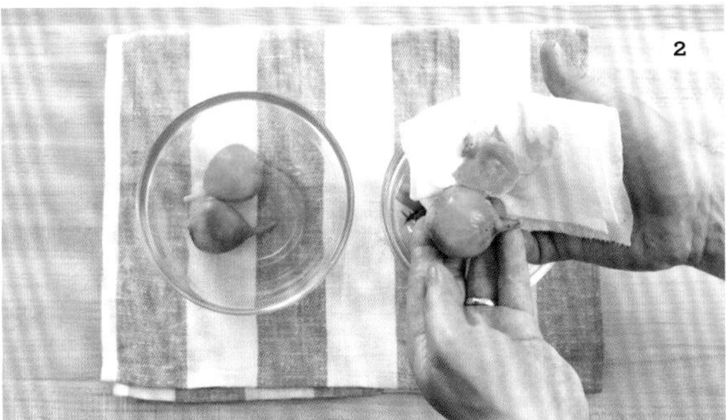

1 Cook the rice

Heat a small pot of salted water to boiling on high. Add the rice and cook 27 to 30 minutes, or until tender. Drain thoroughly and return to the pot. Set aside.

2 Cook & peel the beets

While the rice cooks, heat a separate, small pot of salted water to boiling on high. Add the beets and cook 22 to 25 minutes, or until tender when pierced with a fork. Drain the beets thoroughly. While still warm, using paper towels and your hands, gently rub the skins off the beets; discard the skins. Cut the beets into wedges and place in a bowl.

3 Prepare the ingredients

While the rice and beets cook, wash and dry the fresh produce. Pick the mint leaves off the stems; discard the stems. Cut off and discard the roots of the scallions; thinly slice the scallions, separating the white bottoms and green tops. Using a peeler, remove the green rind of the lime, avoiding the white pith; mince the rind to get 2 teaspoons of zest. Quarter the lime. Peel, pit and medium dice the avocado; toss with the juice of 2 lime wedges to prevent browning; season with salt and pepper to taste. Finely chop the macadamia nuts and place in a small bowl with the panko breadcrumbs.

4 Coat & cook the cod

Season the cod with salt and pepper on both sides. Place the panko-macadamia nut mixture onto a plate and coat 1 side of each seasoned cod fillet in the mixture. In a medium pan (nonstick, if you have one), heat 2 teaspoons of olive oil on medium-high until hot. Add the coated cod, crusted-side first, and cook 2 to 4 minutes per side, or until the crust is golden brown and the fish is cooked through.

5 Finish & plate your dish

Add the cooked beets, white parts of the scallions, half the green parts of the scallions, seasoned avocado, mint (thinly slicing before adding) and the juice of the remaining lime wedges to the cooked rice. Drizzle with olive oil and season with salt and pepper to taste; stir until combined. To plate your dish, divide the dressed rice between 2 dishes. Top each with a piece of cod. Garnish with the remaining green parts of the scallions.

Chicken & Chestnut Pasta

with Cabbage, Chestnuts & Granulated Honey

Italians know chestnuts. Before the introduction of maize to the Old World, chestnut meal was the base of polenta. Chestnut meal—"farina dolce," or "sweet flour," in Italian—was also used to make bread, biscuits and flat cakes. Over the centuries, ingredients changed (chestnut meal was replaced by corn in polenta and yeasty, rising dough in bread), but tastes didn't. There's nothing like chestnut to add earthy flavor and crunchy texture, as you'll see in this recipe for Italian fettuccine pasta and honey-rosemary chicken.

MAKES 2 SERVINGS • ABOUT 700 CALORIES PER SERVING

Ingredients

3 Ounces Chestnuts
2 Carrots
2 Cloves Garlic
2 Sprigs Rosemary
2 Stalks Celery
1 Yellow Onion
¼ Head Savoy Cabbage
10 Ounces Ground Chicken
8 Ounces Fresh Chestnut Fettuccine Pasta
2 Tablespoons Butter
2 Teaspoons Granulated Honey
¼ Cup Grated Pecorino Romano Cheese

1

2

3

4

5

1 Prepare the ingredients
Wash and dry the fresh produce. Heat a large pot of salted water to boiling on high. Roughly chop the chestnuts. Peel the carrots and halve lengthwise; then thinly slice. Peel and thinly slice the garlic. Pick the rosemary leaves off the stems; discard the stems and finely chop the leaves. Thinly slice the celery. Peel and small dice the onion. Remove and discard the core of the cabbage; thinly slice the leaves.

2 Cook the chicken
In a large pan, heat 2 teaspoons of olive oil on medium-high until hot. Add the chicken and cook, stirring occasionally and breaking the chicken apart with a spoon, 4 to 6 minutes, or until lightly browned; season with salt and pepper. Transfer to a bowl and set aside.

3 Cook the aromatics
In the same pan used to cook the chicken, add the onion, carrots, celery, garlic and rosemary; season with salt and pepper. Cook, stirring occasionally, 5 to 7 minutes, or until softened and fragrant.

4 Add the cabbage, chestnuts & chicken
Add the cabbage, chestnuts and cooked chicken to the pan of aromatics. Cook, stirring frequently, 3 to 4 minutes, or until the cabbage wilts and the chestnuts are warmed through.

5 Finish & plate your dish
While the vegetables and chicken cook, add the fresh pasta to the pot of boiling water. Cook 2 to 3 minutes, or until al dente (still firm to the bite). Drain thoroughly and transfer the cooked pasta directly to the pan of vegetables and chicken, reserving 1 cup of the pasta water. Add the butter, granulated honey, all but a pinch of the Pecorino cheese and ½ cup of the reserved pasta water. Cook, stirring to thoroughly coat the noodles, 1 to 2 minutes, or until well combined. (If the sauce seems too dry, slowly add the remaining reserved pasta water until you achieve your desired consistency.) Season with salt and pepper to taste. Remove from heat. To plate your dish, divide the finished pasta between 2 dishes. Garnish with the remaining Pecorino cheese.

Spices

FIELD GUIDE TO SPICES

The following are some of our favorite varieties from around the world. If you can't find them in your local grocery store, check out the nearest spice shop or specialty foods store.

Aleppo Pepper: Reminiscent of cumin. Named for Aleppo, a city on the Silk Road. Bright, moderate kick, with heat building slowly.

Allspice: An essential Caribbean spice. Given its name in the early 17th Century by the English, who thought it tasted like cloves, cinnamon and nutmeg.

Cardamom: In the ginger family. Native to India. Extremely flavorful and peppery, with hints of citrus.

Cinnamon: A timeless spice beloved in classical times. Made from the bark of trees, full of aromatic oils. Wonderfully versatile.

Fenugreek: A delicate, flowering plant used in traditional Indian cooking. The leaves are at once an herb and a vegetable, while its seeds are a spice.

Juniper Berry: A berry look-alike that is actually the cone of the juniper tree. Intensely flavorful. Traditionally used to season wild birds.

Mace: Similar to nutmeg. Both come from the same tree, indigenous to Indonesia: *Myristica fragrans*. More complex, but less sweet.

Mustard Seed: Rustically aromatic and deliciously pungent. Mixing with water releases its kick.

Nigella Seed: Used in Middle Eastern and Indian cuisine. Dry-roasted and used to flavor curries. Sometimes, incorrectly, called "black cumin."

Nutmeg: Highly sought-after since the Middle Ages. Until the 19th Century, all nutmeg was produced on a single, Indonesian island.

Piment d'Espelette: A chile pepper grown in the commune of Espelette, in the French Basque region. Complex heat, with a fruity, briny tang.

Saffron: One of the most beautiful spices. Made from the crimson stigmas of a violet flower. At once grassy, metallic and honeyed in flavor.

Szechuan Peppercorn: Despite its name, not related to black peppercorn or even chile pepper. The hot berry of a plant in the citrus family.

Tellicherry Peppercorn: Regarded as the finest of all peppers. Peppercorns are the tiny, dried dark-red fruit of the *Piperaceae* vine.

Turmeric: Native to Southeast India. Needs high temperatures and significant rainfall to grow. Brilliant golden-yellow. Peppery and bitter.

Vanilla: A jasmine orchid. Indigenous to Central America. Long cultivated by pre-Colombian peoples. Its seed pods are the source of the spice.

THIS IS THE season of spice. The air is almost tinged with the warm fragrance of cloves, cinnamon, nutmeg and ginger. As the days get shorter and the nights get colder, the bounty of the earth begins to ebb. In other seasons, we would turn to fresh, leafy herbs for flavor. In winter, we turn to spices for that little something extra.

We can rely on spices—even if it's hard to pin down their technical definition! In general, spices are long-lasting and powerful ingredients. They are the flavorful seeds, flowers, roots or fruits of plants, often dried to withstand transport. Some spices, like cinnamon, are even made from tree bark and are harvested all year long.

The ability of spices to retain their essence when dried is crucial to their importance. During the height of the spice trade, chefs the world over were introduced to new and exciting ingredients. Incredible things happen when chefs are given new tastes to play with. The mysteriousness that accompanied these spices was soon unveiled and the flavors were thoroughly adopted. Italian béchamel sauce includes its signature sprinkle of nutmeg. Saffron threads from Persia are indispensable to the Spanish paella.

In this chapter, we celebrate the spice rack: to the new flavors it brought us, to the classic flavors we never forget and to the season that could use their warmth and fragrance most of all.

Roasted Butternut Squash

with Stewed White Beans, Gremolata & Brussels Sprouts

Curry powder, though its flavor profile is distinct, isn't a single ingredient. The term itself is a Western invention and can refer to a multitude of spice blends. Most of the curry powder you'll find is a combination of coriander, turmeric, cumin, fenugreek and various chiles. In this dish, you'll use their intermingling savory tastes to season a delicious white bean stew. And as a finishing touch, you'll top the dish with a fresh, zesty gremolata. This versatile mixture of citrus zest, herbs and fresh garlic can be used to add brightness to almost anything. Here, it's the perfect complement to tender, naturally sweet squash, fresh, crunchy Brussels sprouts and a hearty white bean stew.

MAKES 2 SERVINGS • ABOUT 525 CALORIES PER SERVING

Ingredients

1 15-Ounce Can Cannellini Beans
3-4 Sprigs Parsley
2 Pounds Butternut Squash (About ½ Squash)
1 Shallot
2 Cloves Garlic
1 Medium Carrot
1 Lemon
¼ Pound Brussels Sprouts
1 Teaspoon Mild Curry Powder

1 **Prepare the ingredients**
Preheat the oven to 500°F. Wash and dry the fresh produce. Drain and rinse the beans. Pick the parsley leaves off the stems; discard the stems and finely chop the leaves. Using a sturdy, sharp knife, peel and halve the squash. Scoop out and discard the seeds. Cut the squash into ½-inch-thick planks. Peel and mince the shallot and garlic; using the side of your knife, smash the garlic until it resembles a paste. Peel and small dice the carrot. Using a peeler, remove the yellow rind of the lemon, avoiding the white pith; mince the rind to get 2 teaspoons of lemon zest. Quarter the lemon and remove the seeds. Cut off and discard the roots of the Brussels sprouts. Remove and discard the tough outer leaves of the Brussels sprouts. Pick off the remaining leaves until you reach the core of the sprout; place the tender leaves in a bowl and discard the cores.

2 **Cook the squash**
Place the squash on a sheet pan and drizzle with olive oil. Season with salt and pepper and toss to thoroughly coat. Arrange in a single, even layer and roast, flipping halfway through, 20 to 23 minutes, or until golden brown and tender when pierced with a knife.

3 **Make the gremolata**
While the squash roasts, in a small bowl, combine the lemon zest, parsley and half the garlic paste. Stir in enough olive oil to create a rough paste and season with salt and pepper to taste.

4 **Cook the beans**
While the squash continues to roast, in a large pan, heat 2 teaspoons of olive oil on medium until hot. Add the shallot and remaining garlic paste. Cook, stirring frequently, 30 seconds to 1 minute. Add the carrot; season with salt and pepper. Cook, stirring occasionally, 2 to 3 minutes, or until softened. Stir in the curry powder and cook, stirring frequently, 30 seconds to 1 minute, or until toasted. Add the beans and ½ cup of water; season with salt and pepper. Cook, stirring occasionally, 4 to 6 minutes, or until slightly reduced in volume. Remove from heat. Using a fork, mash one-fourth of the beans against the side of the pan; stir to incorporate.

5 **Dress the Brussels sprouts & plate your dish**
In a large bowl, combine the Brussels sprouts, the juice of 1 lemon wedge and a drizzle of olive oil; season with salt and pepper to taste and toss to coat. Just before plating, stir the juice of 1 lemon wedge and half the gremolata into the beans. Divide the roasted squash, beans and Brussels sprouts between 2 dishes. Garnish with the remaining gremolata; serve with the remaining lemon wedges.

Acorn Squash Tempura Tacos

with Spanish Smoked Paprika & Lime Sauce

Squash and spice are a match made in heaven. For these hearty, vegetarian tacos, we added smoked Spanish paprika to the tempura batter and also used it in a tart, smoky dipping sauce. Paprika, though closely associated with cuisines the world over, is made from a chile plant native to the Americas. Peppers were brought back to Spain, flourished and continued to develop. Today, their lightly spicy flavor is fine and nuanced. We love its smokiness, which complements the savory, slightly sweet flavor of these tempura tacos.

MAKES 2 SERVINGS • ABOUT 700 CALORIES PER SERVING

Ingredients

5-6 Sprigs Cilantro
1 Clove Garlic
1 Lime
1 Avocado
1 Small Red Onion
½ Acorn Squash (About 1½ Pounds)
1 Cup Rice Flour
2 Tablespoons Mayonnaise
2 Teaspoons Smoked Spanish Paprika
8 White Corn Tortillas (About 6-Inch Diameter)
2 Ounces Queso Fresco

1 **Prepare the ingredients**
Wash and dry the fresh produce. Pick the cilantro leaves off the stems. Peel and mince the garlic; using the side of your knife, smash until it resembles a paste. Cut the lime into 6 wedges. Pit, peel and slice the avocado; toss with the juice of 1 lime wedge to prevent browning. Peel and very thinly slice the onion. Scoop out and discard the seeds of the acorn squash, then cut lengthwise into ¼-inch-thick wedges.

2 **Coat the squash & make the paprika-lime sauce**
Add ¼ cup of the rice flour to the squash slices and season with salt and pepper. Toss to thoroughly coat. In a small bowl, combine the garlic paste, mayonnaise, half the smoked paprika and the juice of 2 lime wedges. Stir until blended and season with salt and pepper to taste.

3 **Make the rice batter**
In a medium bowl, whisk together the remaining rice flour, the remaining paprika and ¾ cup of water until it forms a thin batter. (As the batter stands, it may thicken. You may need to add up to ¼ cup of additional water to maintain the thin batter consistency.) Season with salt and pepper.

4 **Cook the squash**
In a large pan, heat a ¼-inch layer of olive oil on medium-high until hot, but not smoking. (The oil is hot enough when a small drop of batter sizzles immediately when added to the pan.) Working in batches, dip the floured squash wedges into the rice flour batter to completely coat. Let any excess batter drip off, then very carefully add the battered squash wedges to the hot oil. Cook 1 to 2 minutes per side, or until crispy and golden brown. Transfer to a paper towel-lined plate and immediately season with salt.

5 **Warm the tortillas & plate your dish**
Heat a medium, dry pan on medium until hot. Working in batches, add the tortillas and heat 30 seconds to 1 minute per side, or until soft and pliable. To plate your dish, make 4 tacos with 2 tortillas layered on top of each other for each. Spread a layer of the paprika-lime sauce onto each taco. Divide the tempura-fried acorn squash between the tacos. Top each with avocado and red onion. Crumble the queso freso over the top. Garnish with the cilantro and remaining lime wedges.

New York's Spice Shop: Dual Specialty Store

DOWN A SHORT staircase off of New York City's bustling 1st Ave, there's an oasis. Dual Specialty Store, one of the finest purveyors of spice in the city, has been selling the world's best—and often, rarest—flavors for almost 20 years.

Walking through the door is a transportive experience. Incredible aromas create a dream-like air. And far from being confusing to the senses, a certain harmony exists within these walls.

"This wasn't always a spice shop," says Abdul Patwary, Dual's founder. "Originally, we sold fish, and spices on the side." As the ever-mercurial Manhattan neighborhood changed, customers became increasingly interested in the spices themselves. Dual responded by changing its focus, importing more and more of them.

In 1995, a fire devastated the shop, destroying almost everything. This tragic event only hastened Dual's makeover. What emerged is what exists today, a paradisal vision full of the mystery, excitement and seductive power of spices.

The shelves are stacked with dried herbs from far-flung corners of the map. From Asia to Europe to pre-Colombian America, Dual offers customers a full spectrum of dried spices. But they stock fresh ingredients, too. Their fresh galangal, taro, curry leaves and turmeric are just the beginning.

Mr. Patwary sums it up: "Sometimes, customers come in searching for something specific. They find it here. But, when someone comes in looking for something and finds something unexpected that they'll use for the first time, that's what really makes me smile. That's magic."

DUAL
New Mexican CHIL
Whole
Organic Elder
SAGE

North African Spiced Shrimp
with Couscous

The quintessential North African flavor of this dish comes from a special spice combination called ras el hanout. Literally translated to "head of the shop," ras el hanout was traditionally a blend of the finest spices a purveyor had to offer. Though the specific combinations in ras el hanout vary, you'll usually find coriander, cumin, allspice, cardamom, ginger, black pepper and turmeric. You'll notice the transformative qualities of this wide-ranging spice when searing your shrimp.

MAKES 2 SERVINGS • ABOUT 650 CALORIES PER SERVING

Ingredients

10 Ounces Peeled, Deveined Shrimp
1 Tablespoon Ras El Hanout
4 Cloves Garlic
3 Ounces Baby Spinach
3-4 Prunes
4-5 Pitted Dates
¼ Cup Almonds, Raw & Whole
3-4 Sprigs Parsley
1 Medium Carrot
1 Small Red Onion
1 Lemon
1 Cup Couscous
1 8-Ounce Can Tomato Sauce

1 Prepare the ingredients

Wash and dry the fresh produce. Place the shrimp in a medium bowl and drizzle with olive oil. Sprinkle in the ras el hanout and season with salt and pepper; toss to coat. Set aside to marinate. Peel and mince the garlic. Roughly chop the spinach, prunes, dates and almonds. Pick the parsley leaves off the stems; discard the stems. Peel and small dice the carrot and onion. Quarter the lemon and remove the seeds.

2 Make the couscous & toast the almonds

In a small pot, heat 1 cup of water and a pinch of salt to boiling on high. Once boiling, stir in the couscous and remove from heat. Cover and let stand for 4 to 5 minutes, or until the water is absorbed. Fluff the finished couscous with a fork. Heat a medium, dry pan on medium-high until hot. Add the almonds and toast, stirring frequently, 1 to 2 minutes, or until browned and fragrant. Transfer the toasted almonds to a bowl; wipe out the pan.

3 Cook the aromatics

In a large pan, heat 2 teaspoons of olive oil on medium-high until hot. Add the garlic, carrot and onion; season with salt and pepper. Cook, stirring occasionally, 3 to 5 minutes, or until softened.

4 Finish the couscous

Add the spinach to the pan of vegetables and season with salt and pepper. Cook, stirring frequently, 30 seconds to 1 minute, or until wilted. Add the tomato sauce, cooked couscous, dates, prunes, almonds, half the parsley (roughly chopping just before adding) and ¼ cup of water. Add a drizzle of olive oil and season with salt and pepper to taste. Cook 2 to 3 minutes, or until heated through. Remove from heat and stir in the juice of 2 lemon wedges. Set aside in a warm place.

5 Cook the shrimp & plate your dish

In the same pan used to toast the almonds, heat 2 teaspoons of olive oil on medium-high until hot. Add the coated shrimp and cook, stirring occasionally, 2 to 3 minutes per side, or until cooked through and opaque. Remove from heat and top with the juice of the remaining lemon wedges. To plate your dish, divide the couscous mixture between 2 dishes and top with the shrimp. Garnish with the remaining parsley.

Butternut Squash Mac & Cheese

with Crispy Sage

Cinnamon is fairly unique in the spice world. It's made from the inner bark of an aromatic evergreen tree. Cinnamon is stripped off the tree in long sheets and curls as it dries, forming the cinnamon sticks we're familiar with. As a spice, it has been known since antiquity. (The Egyptians imported it over 2,000 years ago and regarded it as a gift fit for a king.) The spice trade spread it throughout Europe, where its versatile flavor was absorbed by many different culinary traditions. In France it was used to add a signature, warm flavor to béchamel, which is exactly how we're using it here.

MAKES 3 SERVINGS • ABOUT 555 CALORIES PER SERVING

Ingredients

2 Sprigs Sage
½ Butternut Squash (About 1¼ Pound)
2 Tablespoons Butter
2 Tablespoons Whole Wheat Flour
1 Cup Low-Fat Milk
¼ Teaspoon Cinnamon
8 Ounces Whole Wheat Penne Pasta, Dried
½ Cup Grated Parmesan Cheese
¼ Cup Whole Wheat Breadcrumbs

1 Prepare the ingredients

Preheat the oven to 425°F. Heat a medium pot of salted water to boiling on high. Pick the sage leaves off the stems; discard the stems. Peel and medium dice the butternut squash.

2 Crisp the sage

In a large pan, melt the butter on medium-high. Once melted, add the sage leaves and cook, occasionally flipping the leaves, 1 to 2 minutes, or until dark green and crispy. (If your butter starts to burn, reduce the heat to medium-low.) Transfer the sage to a paper towel-lined plate, leaving the butter in the pan. Season the sage leaves with salt and pepper.

3 Make the béchamel sauce

Sprinkle the whole wheat flour into the butter and whisk until combined. Cook on medium-high heat, stirring frequently, 1 to 2 minutes, or until golden, toasted and fragrant. Slowly whisk in the milk until no lumps remain. Reduce the heat to low and season with salt and pepper. Simmer 2 to 4 minutes, stirring until the sauce starts to thicken. Remove from heat.

4 Cook then mash the butternut squash

While the sauce simmers, add the butternut squash to the pot of boiling water. Cook 7 to 9 minutes, or until very soft when pierced with a fork. Using a slotted spoon, transfer the squash to the béchamel sauce, leaving the water boiling in the pot. Using a whisk or fork, mash the squash into the sauce until thoroughly combined. Stir in the cinnamon; season with salt to taste.

5 Cook the pasta & finish your dish

Add the penne and a big pinch of salt to the water used to cook the squash. Cook 13 to 15 minutes, or until al dente. Reserve and set aside ½ cup of the pasta water; drain the pasta thoroughly. Transfer the drained penne, reserved pasta water and the Parmesan cheese to the béchamel-squash mixture. Stir until well combined. Transfer the béchamel-squash-penne mixture into a 10-inch by 7-inch baking dish. In a small bowl, drizzle the breadcrumbs with a little olive oil to slightly moisten; season with salt and pepper to taste. Sprinkle the moistened crumbs in a single layer over the casserole. Bake 5 to 7 minutes, or until golden brown and bubbly. Let stand for 3 minutes before serving. Crumble the crispy sage over the top.

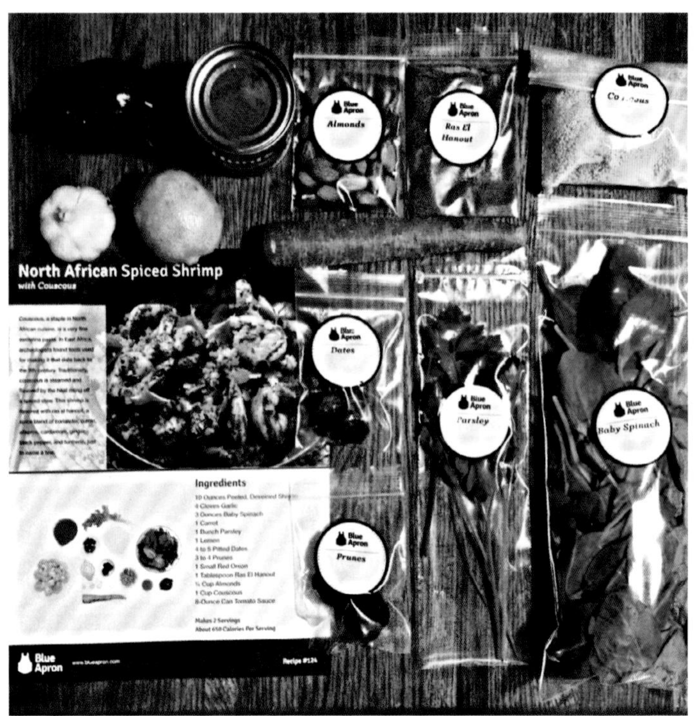

#BLUEAPRON

From the Kitchens of Our Home Chefs

5-Spice Pork Buns
Perishable
Blue Apron
ingredients
reat recipes
Chicken Sloppy Joe Sliders
Blue Apron
Blue Apron

Weekend Projects

In this chapter, you'll actually be *creating* ingredients. They're extremely versatile, as are the techniques you'll use to make them. Later, in our "Feasts with Friends" chapter, you'll put them to use. Let's redefine "home-made."

How To Make Preserved Citrus

Strange as it may seem, wintertime is when citrus is at its ripest. And though it may only grow in temperate climates, the subtle change in weather brings with it juiciness and sweetness. In this recipe, you'll be creating a truly unique ingredient—and the process is completely straightforward. Like most preservation techniques, it relies on a simple ratio. Here, it's one fruit to one tablespoon of sugar and one tablespoon of salt. This simple equation does incredible things. In addition to extending the shelf-life of your citrus, the brine extracts the essence and moisture of the fruit, tames the bitterness of the white pith and softens the rind, making it completely edible and delicious. Preserved citrus is most popular in Indian and North African cuisines, but its applications are boundless. It can be used to put a unique spin on all kinds of salad dressings, dips, pastas, stews—the list goes on. Here, we're using lemons, though this technique can be applied to grapefruits, oranges and limes as well. Experiment by adding spices to the mixture and tailoring the recipe to your own taste. Coriander seeds, cloves, bay leaves, a cinnamon stick and cardamom pods make great additions. Unleash your creativity—and the true flavor of citrus.

Ingredients
5 Lemons
1 12-Ounce Jar
5 Tablespoons Granulated Sugar
5 Tablespoons Kosher or Sea Salt
Approximately 1 Cup Additional Lemon Juice

1 **Prepare the ingredients**
Wash the lemons, scrubbing with a stiff brush to thoroughly clean; dry the lemons. Wash and dry the jar. Make four lengthwise cuts in each of the lemons, as if you were quartering them, but don't cut through to the stem. (The cut lemons should remain intact on one end.)

2 **Stuff the lemons**
Stuff the lemons with the sugar and salt by carefully packing the four incisions, reserving a small amount of sugar and salt. Rub the reserved sugar and salt into the rinds. Place the stuffed lemons into the jar, pressing the lemons down to tightly pack. Top with any leftover sugar and salt.

3 **Let stand at room temperature**
Let the jarred lemons stand at room temperature, occasionally turning the jar on its head to distribute the mixture, for 3 to 5 days. Open the jar and press the lemons down. Add the additional lemon juice to submerge the lemons entirely. Reseal the jar.

4 **Use & enjoy**
Place the jar of lemons in the refrigerator for at least 3 weeks, or until the rinds have softened. (They longer they sit, the better the flavor will be.) Before using, rinse the preserved lemons to remove any excess sugar and salt. Remove and discard the seeds.

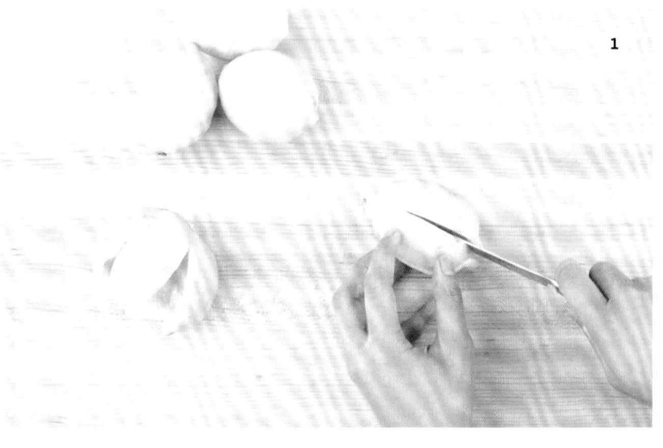
1

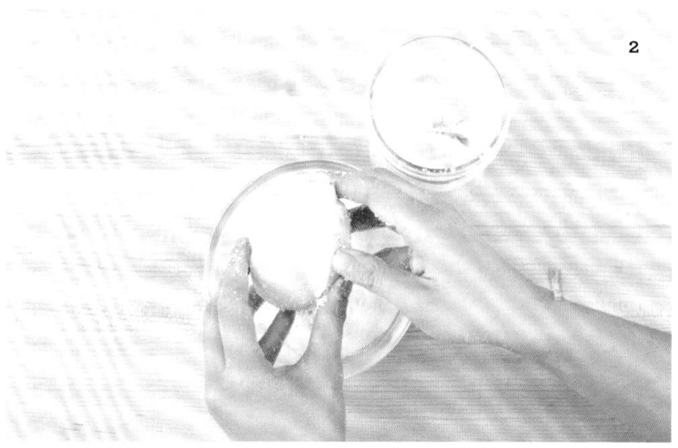
2

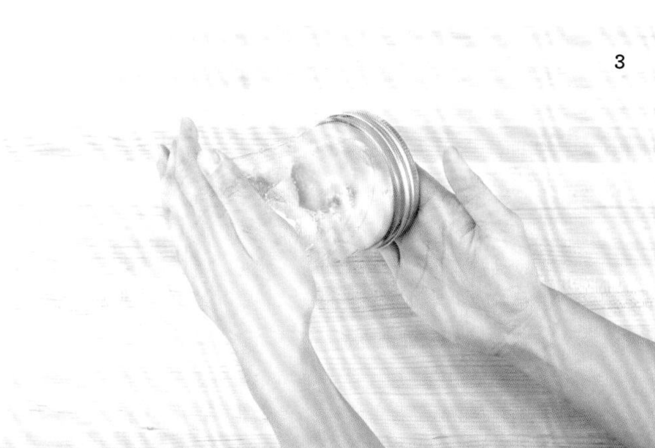
3

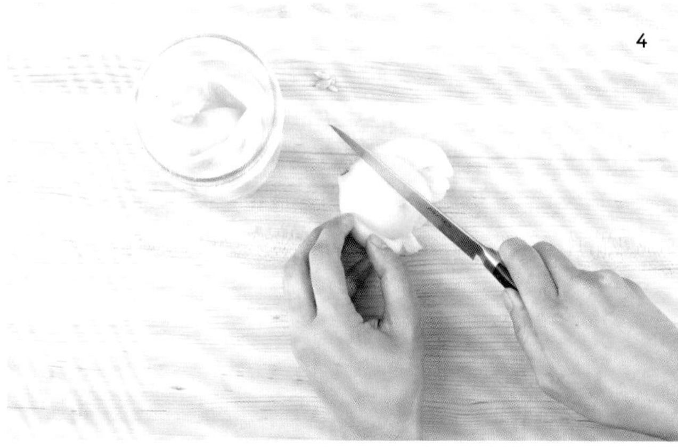
4

Project No. Two

Basic Bread Dough

Bread is one of the oldest human foods. Since the dawn of agriculture, breads of all kinds—flat, risen, sweet, savory—have been feeding populations. In fact, bread has played such an important role in human history that it is present in the basic structure of the English language: the words "company" and "companion," at their root, mean "those who share or eat bread with you." ("Pan" and "com" come from the Latin words for "bread" and "with.") Here, we're sharing a delicious, mildly sweet dough with you. It's wonderful for a variety of uses. In "Feast with Friends," we use it twice: once for dinner rolls served with Roasted Pork Loin (p. 132), and again for cinnamon rolls in Brunch (p. 140). Both of those recipes are provided here. But the dough can be used for anything from pretzels to monkey bread. Have fun with it! Fill it with savory herbs to offset its lightly sugary kick. Roll it with sugar and spices, bake it and drizzle it with confectionery toppngs for a sweet, light treat. And whatever you do, invite friends, family and loved ones—to share, and to eat.

Basic Bread Dough

MAKES 1 POUND OF DOUGH

Ingredients
½ Cup Whole Milk
¼-Ounce Package Active Dry Yeast (About 2¼ Teaspoons)
⅓ Cup Sugar plus 1 Teaspoon
4 Tablespoons Butter, Melted
1 Egg
2¾ Cup All-Purpose Flour (Plus a Little Extra for Dusting)

1 **Bloom the yeast**
In a small pot, warm the milk and ½ cup of water on low heat until it reaches 100-110°F. (Watch carefully to avoid scalding.) Sprinkle in the yeast with 1 teaspoon of sugar. Remove from heat. Let stand for at least 10 minutes, or until foamy.

2 **Make the dough**
In a medium bowl, combine the flour, sugar and ¾ teaspoon of salt. In a large bowl, combine the bloomed yeast (and milk), melted butter and egg. Gradually add the flour mixture to the yeast mixture, gently stirring with a wooden spoon or a spatula, until a thick dough forms.

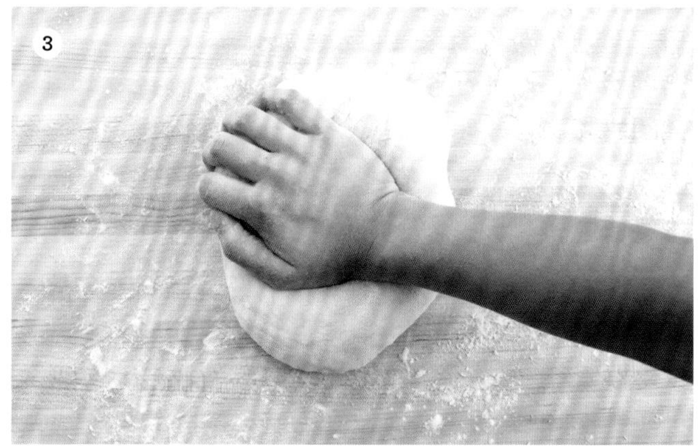

3 **Knead the dough**
Lightly flour a clean, dry work surface and transfer the dough onto it. Using your hands, knead for 5 to 7 minutes, or until smooth, soft and slightly elastic. Shape into a ball.

4 **Finish the dough**
Lightly grease a large bowl with olive oil. Place the kneaded dough into the bowl; turn the dough over a couple of times to coat it in oil. Cover the bowl and set aside in a warm place. Let the dough rise for 45 to 60 minutes, or until it has doubled in size. Punch it down and transfer it to a floured work surface.

Dinner Rolls

MAKES 12 ROLLS

Ingredients

1 Basic Bread Dough (p. 128)
2 Tablespoons Butter, Melted

1 Roll & bake

Preheat the oven to 375°F. Separate the dough into 12 equal portions; roll into balls. Set into a greased baking pan. Cover and let rise 30 to 45 minutes. Uncover and brush the tops with melted butter. Bake 30 to 40 minutes or until golden brown and baked through.

Cinnamon Buns

MAKES 12 BUNS

Ingredients

1 Basic Bread Dough (p. 128)
¼ Cup Butter, Melted
1 Cup Light Brown Sugar
2 Tablespoons Ground Cinnamon
4 Ounces Cream Cheese, Softened
2 Tablespoons Butter, Softened
1 Cup Powdered Sugar
1 Teaspoon Vanilla Extract

1 Prepare the dough

Preheat the oven to 375°F. Coat the bottom of a 13-inch by 9-inch baking pan with butter. Lightly flour a clean, dry work surface. Using a rolling pin or wine bottle, roll the dough into an 11-inch by 15-inch rectangle. Spread the melted butter all over the dough. Evenly sprinkle the brown sugar and cinnamon on top. Roll the dough, then cut crosswise into 12 equal slices.

2 Bake the buns

Place the cinnamon roll slices, side by side and close together, into the pan, with one of the spiral sides up. Lightly cover and let rise until doubled, about 45 minutes to 1 hour. Bake, rotating halfway through, 25 to 35 minutes, or until browned.

3 Finish & glaze the buns

While the buns bake, in a medium bowl, whisk the cream cheese and softened butter until smooth. Gradually whisk in the powdered sugar until smooth. Stir in the vanilla extract and 2 tablespoons of milk. (If necessary, continue to add hot milk, until you have achieved your desired consistency.) Once the cinnamon buns have finished baking, let cool slightly. Spread the glaze over the rolls.

Feasts *with friends*

The following recipes are designed for gatherings, to warm the season with food that's as amazing and comforting as the company you share it with.

Roasted Pork Loin

with Handmade Gnocchi & Fennel, Walnut & Escarole Salad

Roasted pork loin is one of the most majestic winter meals imaginable. Here, we use Frenched, bone-in racks that are as beautiful as they are impressive in taste. Before roasting, you'll butterfly the meat (slice it lengthwise), fill it with a stuffing made from chestnuts, figs and aromatic herbs, then tie it up. The stuffing's complex, powerful flavors infuse the chops, leaving them tender, juicy and simply fit for kings and queens. But no royal feast would be complete without a trio of exquisite side dishes. Here, we're offering up pillowy, homemade gnocchi. Hand-rolled until the dough just comes together and yields to the slighest touch, cut small and finished in gorgonzola cheese sauce, the dish's richness is perfectly balanced by sweet, crisp forelle pear. A fennel-escarole salad with black walnuts adds tart notes, crunch and beauty on the side. Meanwhile, soft, warm, freshly baked dinner rolls (p. 129) with a sweet-and-salty pop (we topped ours with herbs and salt) are terrific for mopping up the savory, seasoned juices of the pork and the creamy gnocchi sauce. No other meal so thoroughly deserves the moniker "feast."

Make the gnocchi beforehand and freeze (if desired).

Roast the pork loin.

Dress the salad just before serving.

Enjoy!

Roasted Pork Loin

with Chestnut & Fig Stuffing

MAKES 10 TO 12 SERVINGS

Ingredients

8-10 Pounds Pork Loin (Two Whole Frenched Racks)
1 Cup Chestnuts, Roasted & Peeled
1 Cup Dried Figs
1 Head Garlic
1 Leek
3-5 Sprigs Rosemary
3-4 Sprigs Sage
¼ Cup Preserved Citrus (Preferably Orange)
½ Cup Whole Grain Dijon Mustard
2 6-Foot Pieces Butcher's Twine
2 Tablespoons Smooth Dijon Mustard
½ Cup Chicken Demi-Glace

1

2

1 Prepare the ingredients

Preheat the oven to 400°F. Remove the pork from the refrigerator to bring to room temperature. Roughly chop the chestnuts. Remove the fig stems; halve and thinly slice the figs. Peel and mince the garlic; smash with the side of your knife until it resembles a paste. Trim off the roots and

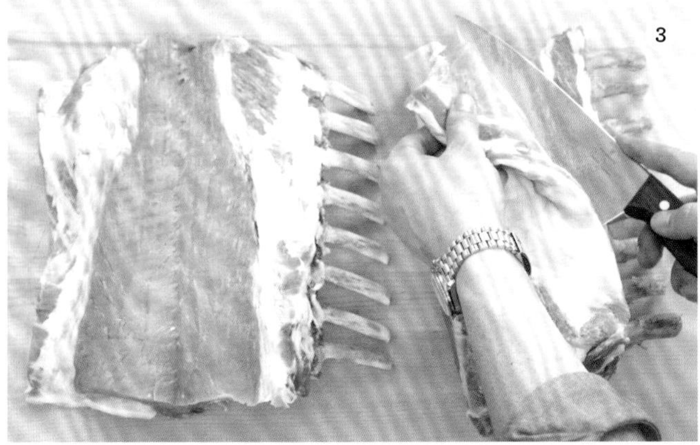

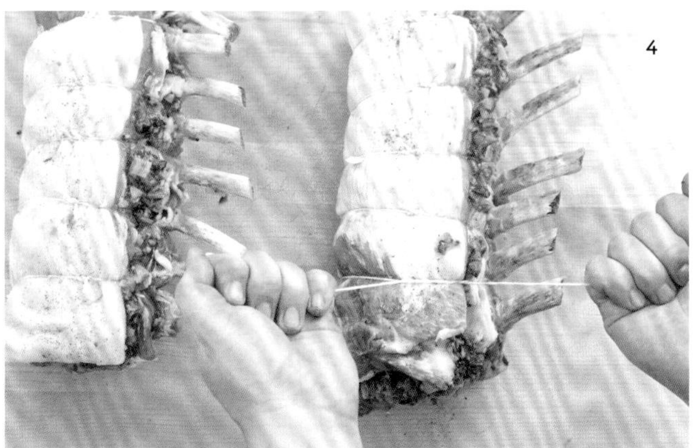

upper, dark-green parts of the leek. Slice the leek in half lengthwise, then thoroughly rinse between the leaves to remove any grit; small dice the leek. Pick the rosemary and sage leaves off the stems; discard the stems. Thinly slice the sage leaves. Mince the rosemary. Roughly chop the preserved citrus.

2 Prepare the stuffing

In a medium pan, heat 2 teaspoons of olive oil on medium-high until hot. Add the garlic and leeks. Cook, stirring occasionally, 3 to 4 minutes, or until softened. Add the chestnuts, figs, rosemary, sage, preserved citrus, whole grain mustard and 1 cup of water. Cook, stirring occasionally, 3 to 4 minutes, or until thoroughly combined and warmed through. Transfer to a bowl and set aside to cool.

3 Butterfly the pork

Lay the pork out on a clean, dry work surface, bone-side down, with the bones facing the hand you hold a knife with. Holding your knife parallel to the work surface, and starting by the bone, carefully slice the pork lengthwise toward the center. Using successive cuts, continue slicing until you reach the middle of the loin, pulling the meat back with your free hand as you go and patting it down. (When the pork is fully butterflied, it should lie flat on the work surface.) Season with salt and pepper.

4 Stuff & tie the pork

Cut each piece of butcher's twine into 5 equal pieces. Spoon the stuffing onto the center of the seasoned, butterflied pork. Wrap the loin back into its original position around the stuffing. Tie the stuffed loin crosswise with the butcher's twine, starting from the center and working your way toward the ends, alternating sides as you go. Use 5 pieces of twine per loin to ensure that it's secure and the stuffing will not fall out as it cooks.

5 Roast the pork

Transfer the tied loins to a roasting pan (with oven-safe rack) and roast 70 to 80 minutes, or until a meat thermometer reaches an internal temperature of 135°F. Transfer the cooked pork to a clean, dry work surface and allow it to rest for at least 15 minutes before carving. Reserve the juices from the roasting pan.

6 Deglaze the pan & make the sauce

While the pork rests, skim off and discard some of the fat from the reserved juices. Transfer the remaining juices to a small pot and whisk in the smooth Dijon mustard, chicken demi-glace and ½ cup of water. Cook on medium, whisking frequently, 4 to 6 minutes, or until slightly thickened; season with salt and pepper to taste. Remove from heat and serve with the pork.

Handmade Potato Gnocchi

with Gorgonzola Dolce, Forelle Pear & Chives

MAKES 10 TO 12 SERVINGS

Ingredients

3 Pounds Russet Potatoes
8 Cloves Garlic
4 Shallots
5 Ounces Gorgonzola Dolce Cheese
1 Large Bunch Chives
1 Lemon
2 Forelle Pears
1 Cup All-Purpose Flour (Plus a Little Extra for Dusting)
2 Eggs
1 Cup Heavy Cream

1 Cook the potatoes

Preheat the oven to 450°F. Wash and dry the fresh produce. Pierce each potato a couple of times on both sides with a fork and place on a sheet pan. Roast in the oven 45 to 60 minutes, or until very tender when pierced with a fork. While still warm, cut each potato in half. Scoop out the interiors of the potatoes; discard the skins or save for another use. Place the potatoes into the hopper of a food mill. Pass through the food mill. Transfer to a large bowl.

2 Prepare the ingredients

While the potatoes cook, peel and mince the garlic and shallots. Using your fingers, tear the cheese into small pieces. Cut the chives into 1-inch pieces. Cut the lemon into 6 wedges; remove the seeds. Core and small dice the pears; toss with the juice of 3 lemon wedges to prevent browning. (Save the remaining lemon wedges for another use.)

3 Make the gnocchi dough

Add the flour and eggs to the milled potatoes. Using a spatula, gently combine the mixture until a rough dough forms, being careful not to overwork it. (This will toughen the dough.) Transfer to a clean, dry work surface and lightly knead for 1 to 2 minutes, or until smooth. (If necessary, lightly flour the work surface to prevent sticking.)

4 Form the gnocchi

Divide the dough into 6 equal portions. Working with 1 portion at a time, roll the dough into ¼-inch-thick logs. Using a knife or a pastry cutter, cut the logs crosswise into ¼-inch pieces and transfer to a sheet pan; thoroughly toss with flour to prevent sticking. Repeat with the remaining dough. (If you are making the gnocchi beforehand, transfer to an airtight container and freeze for up to 1 week.)

5 Make the sauce

Heat a large pot of salted water to boiling on high. In a large pan, heat 1 tablespoon of olive oil on medium-high until hot. Add the garlic and shallots and cook, stirring frequently, 2 to 4 minutes, or until softened and fragrant. Add the pears, cheese and heavy cream; season with salt and pepper. Cook, stirring occasionally, 4 to 6 minutes, or until slightly reduced in volume and thickened.

6 Cook the gnocchi & finish your dish

While the sauce cooks, add the gnocchi to the pot of boiling water, stirring to separate. Cook 3 to 5 minutes, or until tender and the gnocchi float to the top of the pot. Using a slotted spoon or a strainer, transfer the cooked gnocchi to the pan of sauce. (If the pan seems too small, divide the sauce and gnocchi between multiple pans.) Cook 3 to 5 minutes, stirring occasionally, or until the sauce has reduced slightly. Remove from heat and season with salt and pepper to taste. Transfer the finished gnocchi to a serving platter. Garnish with pepper and the chives.

Fennel, Walnut & Escarole Salad

with Lemon-Anchovy Vinaigrette

MAKES 10 TO 12 SERVINGS

Ingredients

2 Fennel Bulbs
2 Heads Escarole
2 Lemons
2 Ounces Parmesan Cheese
1 Bunch Parsley
1 Clove Garlic
½ Cup Black Walnuts, Shelled & Raw
½ Cup Panko Breadcrumbs
1 Tablespoon Smooth Dijon Mustard
1 Teaspoon Anchovy Paste

1 Prepare the ingredients

Wash and dry the fresh produce. Remove and discard the fennel stems and fronds. Thinly slice the fennel bulbs. Cut off and discard the root end of the escarole; roughly chop the leaves. Using a peeler, remove the rind of 1 lemon, avoiding the pith; mince the rind to get 1 tablespoon of zest. Halve both lemons; squeeze the juice into a small bowl and discard the seeds. Using a peeler, shave the cheese. Pick the parsley off the stems; discard the stems. Peel and smash the garlic. Roughly chop the walnuts.

2 Toast the walnuts

Heat a medium pan on medium-high until hot. Add the walnuts and toast, stirring frequently, 4 to 6 minutes, or until fragrant. Transfer to a small bowl and wipe out the pan.

3 Toast the panko breadcrumbs

In the same pan used to toast the walnuts, heat 2 teaspoons of olive oil on medium-high until hot. Add the garlic clove and cook 30 seconds to 1 minute, or until fragrant. Add the breadcrumbs; season with salt and pepper. Cook, stirring frequently, 2 to 4 minutes, or until toasted. Remove from heat; discard the garlic clove.

4 Make the vinaigrette

Add the lemon zest, Dijon mustard and anchovy paste to the lemon juice; season with salt and pepper to taste. Slowly whisk in ½ cup of olive oil until well combined.

5 Finish & serve your dish

In a large bowl, combine the escarole, fennel, parsley and toasted walnuts; season with salt and pepper. Add enough vinaigrette to coat the greens and toss thoroughly to mix. Transfer to a serving platter. Garnish with the Parmesan cheese and toasted breadcrumbs.

FEAST No. TWO

Brunch

While we love dinner, there is always a lingering question: what to do the morning after? There's only one answer: brunch! When you've got a house full of hungry loved ones early in the day, nothing is quite as delicious and satisfying. And, though brunch is quickly becoming a mainstay of American cuisine, it's actually a British tradition. In England, people have been enjoying this meal since at least the late 1800s. Originally, brunch was a Sunday affair, a portmanteau served "postchurch," beginning with coffee or tea and other breakfast fixtures before moving on to heavier, lunch-type fare. In 1895, British journalist Guy Beringer said of the meal, "It makes you satisfied with yourself and your fellow beings." It's the perfect way to bring people together and brighten up the day. Here, we've included a batch of simple, easy brunch recipes—and a timeline to keep you from having to wake up too early.

Make the salmon 2 to 3 days before.

Make the biscuit batter the day before.

Just before serving, make the hollandaise sauce.

Enjoy!

Eggs Benedict

Eggs Benedict is a brunch mainstay. But that doesn't mean there's just one recipe. In fact, the dish has countless variations. So try making your own! The traditional version uses English muffins. Instead, we're using biscuits. Other options include: brioche, cornbread, potato cakes, crispy pita—even crab cakes. The key is choosing a bread that's both chewy and stable, a base that will soak up the egg yolk and silky hollandaise sauce. Next, choose your protein. Canadian bacon is the convention. But we're using gravlax (cured salmon) and pancetta. You can also try chicken sausage or corned beef. Even lobster is a great contender. Poached eggs—let's not mess with those! But hollandaise sauce, too, can be endlessly tailored. Once you have the basic recipe down (provided here), add flavors to suit your taste. Variations include: chipotle hollandaise, lemon hollandaise, lemongrass hollandaise, miso-yuzu hollandaise. Or, if you're so inclined, you can make a whiskey hollandaise for sharpened, smoky flavor. To assemble your dish, cut the biscuit in half. Lay the salmon or pork across the bottom half. (The protein can protrude a little on the sides.) Gently lay a poached egg on top. Drizzle hollandaise sauce on the egg. Top with the upper half of the biscuit to make a sandwich, or serve open-faced and eat with a knife and fork.

Roasted Pancetta

MAKES 10 TO 12 SERVINGS

Ingredients
1 Pound Pancetta, Thinly Sliced

1 **Prepare the ingredients**
Preheat the oven to 450°F. Place a wire rack on top of a sheet pan. Arrange the pancetta in a single, even layer.

2 **Roast the pancetta**
Roast in the oven for 8 to 10 minutes, or until browned and cooked through. Remove from the oven and let cool slightly before serving.

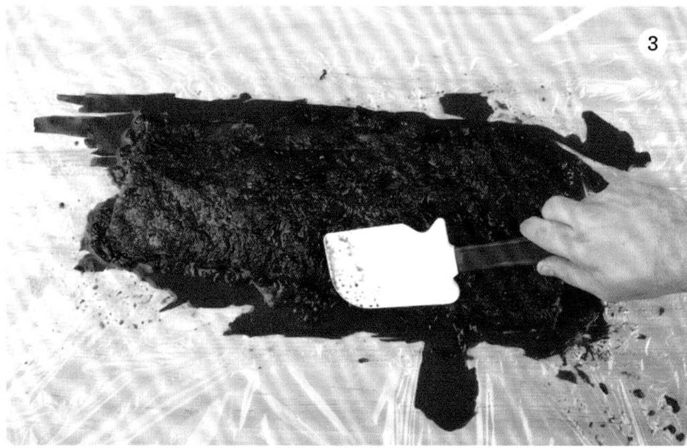

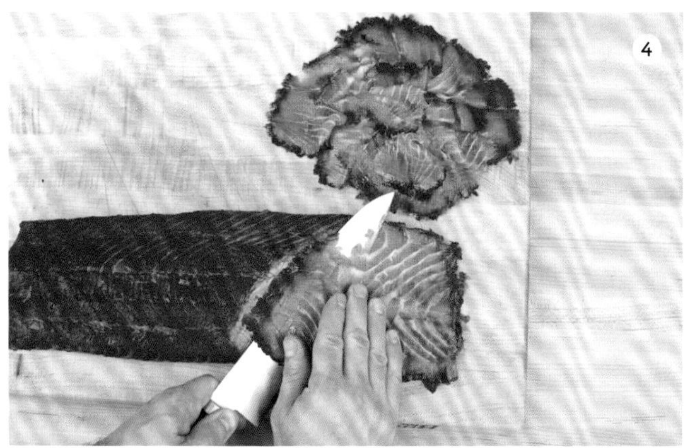

Beet-Cured Gravlax

MAKES 10 TO 12 SERVINGS

Ingredients

2 Large Red Beets, Without Greens (About 1 Pound)
1 Grapefruit
1⅓ Cup Sugar
2 Cups Kosher Salt
4 Pounds Skin-On Salmon (With Pinbones Removed)
¼ Cup Loose Leaf Jasmine Green Tea
1 Small Bunch Chives

1 Prepare the ingredients
Wash and dry the fresh produce. Peel the beets; grate on the large side of a box grater. (Cover your cutting board with plastic wrap to prevent staining.) Using a peeler, remove the rind of the grapefruit, avoiding the white pith; mince the rind to get ¼ cup of zest. Cut the grapefruit in half and squeeze the juice into a small bowl; discard the seeds.

2 Make the gravlax mixture
In a medium bowl, combine the sugar, salt and grapefruit zest and, using your hands, rub together for 30 seconds to 1 minute to activate the essential oils and infuse the sugar and salt. Add the beets and grapefruit juice; stir until well combined.

3 Prepare the salmon
Create a layer of overlapping pieces of plastic wrap, slightly larger than the salmon, on a clean work surface. Spread a thin layer of the gravlax mixture onto the center of the plastic wrap. Lay the salmon on top, skin-side down, and top with the remaining gravlax mixture. Using a spatula, rub the mixture into the salmon. Evenly sprinkle with the green tea. Tightly wrap the coated salmon in plastic wrap to completely seal. Transfer to a sheet pan and place in the refrigerator. Refrigerate for 48 to 72 hours, or until the salmon is a bright fuchsia color and the center of the salmon is somewhat firm.

4 Finish the salmon
When cured, remove and discard the plastic wrap and rinse the salmon under water to remove the curing mixture. Transfer to a cutting board and very thinly slice; transfer to serving platter. Garnish with the chives (finely chopping just before using).

Poached Eggs

MAKES 10 TO 12 SERVINGS

Ingredients
1 Tablespoon White Vinegar or Lemon Juice
2 Dozen Eggs, Preferably as Fresh as Possible
1 Small Bunch Chives

1 **Poach the eggs**
Heat a medium pot of water to boiling on high. Add the vinegar or lemon juice. Reduce the heat until the water is just barely simmering. Working 4 at a time, crack each egg into a separate small bowl. Stir the boiling water to create a swirling whirlpool. Gently add up to 4 eggs at a time to the boiling water, gently stirring to separate. Cook 3 to 5 minutes, or until the egg whites are set and the yolks are still runny.

2 **Store & reheat the eggs**
Using a slotted spoon, remove the poached eggs from the hot water and immediately transfer to a bowl of ice water to stop the cooking process. Store in a bowl of cold water for up to 1 hour, or until ready to use. Just before serving, reheat the poached eggs in a pot of very hot water for a few seconds. Garnish with chives (mincing just before garnishing).

Hollandaise Sauce

MAKES 3 CUPS

Ingredients
6 Large Egg Yolks
3 Tablespoons Lemon Juice
¼ Teaspoon Ground Cayenne (Plus Extra for Garnishing)
2 Cups Butter, Melted

1 **Start the sauce**
Heat a medium pot of water to boiling on high; reduce the heat to low and simmer. Create a double boiler by placing a large heat-safe bowl on top of the pot of boiling water, making sure that the water isn't high enough to touch the bowl. In the large bowl, combine the egg yolks, lemon juice, cayenne pepper and 3 tablespoons of water, whisking until well combined; season with salt. Cook, whisking frequently, 1 to 2 minutes, or until just heated through (over cooking will cause the eggs to scramble).

2 **Finish the sauce**
Turn off the heat. Gradually add the melted butter to the bowl in a slow steady stream, whisking constantly to completely combine and emulsify. Remove from heat and season with salt and pepper to taste. Transfer to a serving dish and garnish with cayenne pepper.

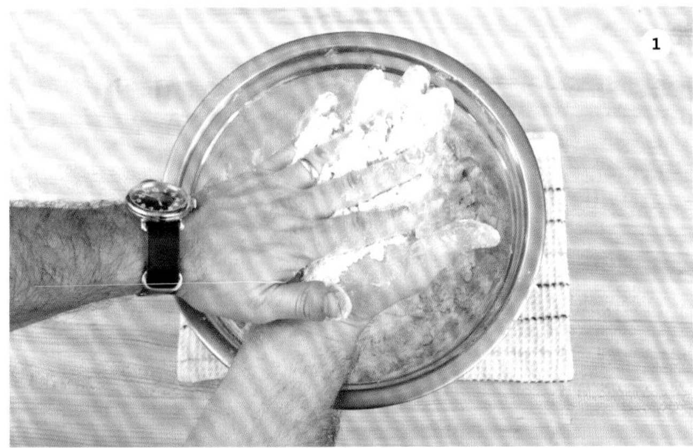

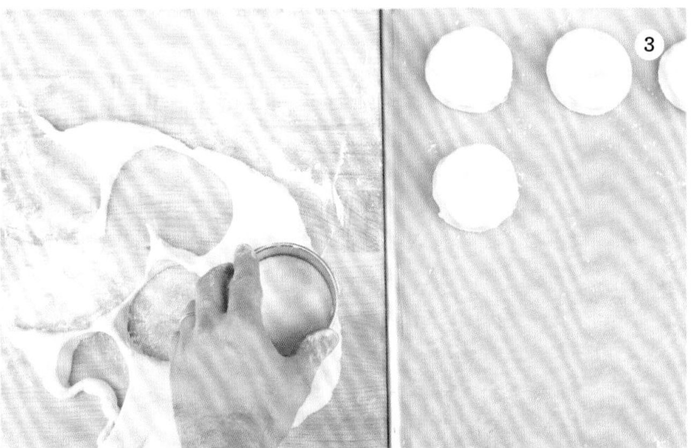

Buttermilk Biscuits

MAKES 12 TO 16 BISCUITS

Ingredients

2½ Cups All-Purpose Flour
4 Teaspoons Baking Powder
¼ Teaspoon Baking Soda
1 Tablespoon Granulated Sugar
10 Tablespoons Cold Butter, Cubed
1 Cup Cold Buttermilk

1 Preheat the oven & start the batter

Preheat the oven to 450°F. Line a sheet pan with parchment paper. In a medium bowl, combine the flour, baking powder, baking soda, sugar and 1¼ teaspoon of salt. Using your hands, "cut" or crumble the butter into the flour mixture by rubbing the butter and flour mixture together until the butter is very thin and evenly distributed.

2 Add the buttermilk

Using a spatula, wooden spoon or your hands, stir in the buttermilk and gently mix just until a dough forms. (Over-mixing will cause it to toughen).

3 Form the biscuits

Place the dough onto a floured surface and roll or press out until about 1-inch thick. Using a biscuit cutter or an inverted drinking cup, cut out twelve 3-inch discs by pressing the cutter straight down as you cut; do not twist the cutter as this compacts and seals the edges of your biscuit, making them less light and flaky.

4 Bake the biscuits

Place the cut-out biscuits on the parchment-lined sheet pan. Bake on the middle rack, turning the pan halfway through, 10 to 14 minutes, or until lightly browned and cooked through. Let cool slightly before serving.

Arugula Salad

with Preserved Lemon Vinaigrette

MAKES 10 TO 12 SERVINGS

Ingredients

1 Lemon
1 Shallot
¼ Cup Preserved Lemon
1 Bunch Mint
5 Ounces Arugula
½ Cup Pistachios, Shelled & Roasted
½ Cup Dried Cranberries

1 **Make the vinaigrette**
Wash and dry the fresh produce. Quarter the lemon and remove the seeds. Peel and mince the shallot and place in a small bowl with the juice of all 4 lemon wedges. Finely chop the preserved lemon and add to the shallot-lemon juice mixture; season the with salt and pepper to taste. Slowly whisk in ¼ cup of olive oil until well combined.

2 **Dress & serve your dish**
Pick the mint leaves off the stems; discard the stems and place the leaves in a large bowl along with the arugula, pistachios and dried cranberries; season with salt and pepper. Just before serving, add enough vinaigrette to coat the greens (you may have extra vinaigrette); toss gently to mix. Transfer to a serving platter.

Desserts

Let's share in the sweetness of the season. Just in time for the holidays, we've created a few treats to give your winter meals a perfect finishing touch (or just to have around as a sweet snack).

Lemon Polenta Cake

Before polenta is paired with savory toppings, it's simply cornmeal. Why not make it sweet? That's exactly what we're doing in this delicious, semi-sweet cake. After rubbing the lemon zest, thyme and sugar together to infuse the sugar with the lemon rind's essential oils and the thyme's fragrance, you'll bake it. And feel free to experiment! This cake can be customized with your favorite citrus fruits and savory herbs.

MAKES 16 SERVINGS

Ingredients

4 Lemons
2 Cups Butter, Unsalted & Softened (Plus ½ Tablespoon for Buttering the Pan)
1 Tablespoon Flour
6 Sprigs Thyme
1½ Cups Fine Ground or Instant Polenta
1½ Teaspoons Baking Powder
2 Cups Sugar
4 Cups Almonds, Ground
2 Teaspoons Vanilla Extract
6 Eggs
¼ Cup Powdered Sugar

1 Prepare the ingredients
Preheat the oven to 350°F. Using a peeler, remove the yellow rind of all 4 lemons, avoiding the white pith; mince the rinds to get 2 tablespoons of zest. Quarter 1 of the lemons and remove the seeds. Thinly slice 1 of the lemons into rounds; remove and discard the seeds. (Save the remaining 2 lemons for another use.) Generously grease the bottom and sides of a 10-inch round pan with butter; then dust with flour, shaking the flour around the pan to coat it. (If desired, line the bottom of the pan with parchment paper to prevent sticking.) Pick the thyme leaves off the stems; discard the stems and roughly chop the leaves. In a small bowl, stir together the polenta, baking powder and ¼ teaspoon salt.

2 Make the lemon-thyme sugar
In a large bowl, combine the sugar, thyme and all but a pinch of the lemon zest. Using your hands, massage the mixture together.

3 Cream the butter & flavored sugar
In a separate bowl or in a standing mixer, cream the butter and lemon-thyme sugar together, until fluffy and pale.

4 Add the wet & dry ingredients
Stir the ground almonds and vanilla into the butter-sugar mixture. Add the eggs one a time, beating after each until thoroughly combined. Stir in the juice of the remaining lemon wedges. Using a spatula or spoon, gently fold the polenta, baking powder and salt into the batter, until well combined.

5 Bake & finish the cake
Transfer the finished batter to the prepared pan. Top with the sliced lemon rounds. Bake 50 to 55 minutes, or until the top is deep brown and a toothpick inserted into the center of the cake comes out clean. Remove from the oven and let cool 10 to 15 minutes. Before removing the cake from the pan, run a knife around the edge to loosen it from the pan. Invert the cake onto a drying rack and then transfer it to a serving platter. Just before serving, using a sifter, lightly dust the top of the cake with the powdered sugar. Garnish with the reserved lemon zest.

Chocolate Pots de Crème

MAKES 10 SERVINGS

Ingredients
1 Vanilla Bean
1 Cup Whole Milk
1½ Cups Heavy Cream
12 Ounces Bittersweet Chocolate
6 Egg Yolks
1 Cup Granulated Sugar
Sea Salt, Optional for Garnishing
¼ Cup Cacao Nibs, Optional for Garnishing

1 Make the chocolate mixture

Preheat the oven to 325°F. Cut the vanilla bean in half lengthwise; using the back of a knife, scrape out and reserve the seeds. In a large bowl, combine the scraped vanilla bean, chocolate, milk and 1 cup of heavy cream. Microwave the mixture on high for 2 to 3 minutes, stirring every 30 seconds, or until thoroughly combined. Set aside.

2 Make the egg base

In a large bowl, combine the egg yolks, sugar and half the reserved vanilla bean seeds. Whisk thoroughly.

3 Make the custard

Slowly add one-third of the chocolate mixture to the egg base; whisk until thoroughly combined. (This process, called tempering, helps to ensure that the eggs won't scramble from the heat of the chocolate mixture.) Whisk in the remaining chocolate mixture; whisk until thoroughly combined. (Be careful not to whisk too vigorously, as that will form air bubbles in the custard.)

4 Bake the custard

Divide the custard mixture between ten 4-ounce ramekins. Place the ramekins into 1 or more high-sided baking dishes and place in the oven. Carefully add 1 inch of water around the base of the ramekins to the baking dishes to create a water bath. Bake the custards for 35 minutes, or until just set.

5 Make the whipped cream & finish your dish

In a large bowl, combine the remaining ½ cup of heavy cream and the reserved vanilla bean seeds. Whip using a large whisk until you achieve stiff peaks. Cover and store in the refrigerator until ready to use. Just before serving, sprinkle each of the custard-filled ramekins with a pinch of sea salt flakes, if you'd like. Top with a large dollop of whipped cream and garnish with the cacao nibs, if you'd like.

Apple Cider Caramels

It's a two-for-one! We're taking full advantage of the season and making a sweet treat with caramel and apple cider. These scrumptious, chewy caramels make a great homemade gift. With caramels, controlling the temperature of the melted sugar is crucial to getting the perfect consistency. Use a candy thermometer and keep a watchful eye. In this recipe we used a little cinnamon to give it holiday warmth, but you can experiment with spices and seasonings. Nutmeg, or even spices like ancho chiles or paprika, make great, unique additions.

MAKES 24 CARAMELS

Ingredients
4 Cups Apple Cider
8 Tablespoons Salted Butter, Cubed
1½ Cups Light Brown Sugar
½ Cup Heavy Cream
½ Teaspoon Ground Cinnamon
Sea Salt (Optional)

Special Equipment
Candy Thermometer

1 Reduce the apple cider
In a medium pot, heat the apple cider to boiling on high. Reduce the heat to low and simmer, 40 to 45 minutes, or until thick, syrupy and reduced in volume to about ½ cup. While the cider reduces, line an 8-inch by 8-inch pan with parchment paper, leaving at least a 1-inch overhang on 2 opposite sides. Once the cider is reduced, turn off the heat. Attach a candy thermometer to the pot.

2 Add the butter, sugar & cream
Stir in the butter, sugar and heavy cream. Cook on medium-high heat for 5 to 10 minutes, or until the candy thermometer reads 260°F.

3 Add the cinnamon & salt
Remove the pot from heat. Add in the cinnamon and ½ teaspoon of salt; stir until well combined.

4 Let the caramels set
Pour the caramel mixture into the prepared pan. Let stand for 2 hours, or until firm.

5 Cut & wrap caramels
Using an oiled knife, cut the caramel into small pieces. Wrap each caramel in 4-inch squares of parchment paper, tightly twisting the ends to seal them. If desired, top each caramel with a pinch of flaky sea salt before wrapping.

Holiday Sugar Cookies

To save time, you can make this dough in advance and refrigerate it for up to 3 days or freeze it for up to 2 weeks. (If you freeze the dough, defrost it in the refrigerator before using.)

MAKES 18 TO 24 COOKIES

Ingredients

2½ Cups All-Purpose Flour, Plus More for Kneading and Rolling the Dough
1 Teaspoon Baking Powder
1 Cup Sugar
1 Cup Butter, Room Temperature
1 Egg
1 Tablespoon Whole Milk
1 Teaspoon Almond Extract
1 Teaspoon Vanilla Extract

1 Prepare the batter
In a small bowl, combine the flour, baking powder and ¼ teaspoon of salt. In a large bowl, cream the sugar and butter together until light and fluffy. Whisk the egg, milk and almond and vanilla extracts into the sugar-butter mixture; beat until fully combined. Using a whisk or spatula, gradually add the flour-baking powder mixture in 3 increments until a dough forms. (If the dough seems too soft for rolling, add up to 1 tablespoon of flour to achieve your desired consistency.)

2 Knead & refrigerate the dough
Lightly dust a clean work surface with flour. Transfer the dough to the prepared surface and, using your hands, knead until smooth. Divide the dough in half and, using your hands or a rolling pin, press or roll into ¼-inch-thick discs. Tightly wrap with plastic wrap or wax paper. Refrigerate for at least 30 minutes, or until firm.

3 Cut out the cookies
Preheat the oven to 350°F. Adjust the oven rack to the middle position. Working one at a time, roll each chilled dough disc to a ¼-inch-thickness; cut into desired shapes using cookie cutters. Place the cut-out shapes on a parchment-lined sheet pan, spacing them about 1½ inches apart. Reroll any remaining dough and continue cutting shapes until all of the dough is used.

4 Bake the cookies
Bake, rotating halfway through, 8 to 10 minutes, or until light golden brown. Repeat with the second portion of rolled dough. Cool on the sheet pan for 2 minutes before transferring to a wire rack to cool to room temperature.

1

2

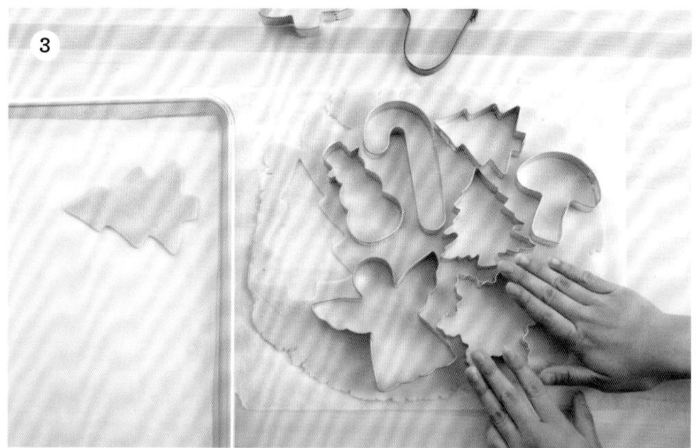
3

4

Cookie Decorating

What would the holidays be without sugar cookies? These favorites are a delicious, buttery sign that it's time to celebrate. So let's decorate! We've outlined four ways to spiff things up and get everyone involved in the process. Before baking, you can create different shapes using cookie cutters, or get adventurous and use multiple cutters to make beautiful imprints. Make your own stencils to create unique cookie shapes or decorative sprinkle patterns. After baking, create a lacy design using not one but two kinds of chocolate drizzles. And of course, there's always the classic icing. When decorating, there are a lot of different choices. When we couldn't find the perfect shade of sprinkle, we made them ourselves by adding a little food coloring to granulated sugar. One drop per tablespoon of sugar did the trick. We also found magical things like edible glitter, edible paint and dragées (small, metallic-colored, edible balls). You can also color your icing with a few drops of food coloring. Whatever your palette, let your inner winter artist out and have some fun!

1

2

3

4

4 Ways to Decorate

1 Imprints or Cutouts
Using a cookie cutter, cut out a cookie from the rolled-out dough. Gently press a slightly smaller cookie cutter (possibly in a different shape) into the cookie, leaving behind its imprint. To create a cutout, press the smaller cookie cutter all the way through the dough and remove the inner shape.

2 Cut Out Stencil with Sprinkles
Cut out cookies from the rolled-out dough using your desired cookie cutter. Using scissors, cut a custom shape (stencil) out of a piece of cardboard or sturdy paper. Lay the stencil on top of the cutout cookie. Sprinkle your desired sprinkles on top of the stencil. Remove the stencil. Transfer the decorated cookie to a sheet pan and bake.

3 Double Chocolate Drizzle
After your cookies are baked, in 2 separate bowls, melt **12 Ounces of Chopped Bittersweet Chocolate** and **12 Ounces of Chopped White Chocolate** in the microwave in 15 to 30 second intervals, stirring between each interval, until melted and smooth. Using a spoon, drizzle each chocolate over each cookie. If desired, top with sprinkles. Let stand for 10 to 15 minutes to set before serving.

4 Icing
After your baked cookies have cooled, in a medium bowl, combine **1 Cup Powdered Sugar** and **4 Teaspoons Whole Milk**, whisking until thoroughly combined. (If the icing seems too thick, slowly add up to an additional tablespoon of milk until you achieve your desired consistency.) Spread the icing onto cookies with a spoon or knife. Alternatively, transfer the icing to plastic sandwich bag and cut off a small corner (or use a pastry bag). Pipe the icing onto the cookies in a decorative pattern.

About Blue Apron

Blue Apron makes incredible home cooking accessible by delivering original recipes and fresh ingredients to customers nationwide.

Chefs around the world wear blue aprons when learning to cook, and the blue apron has become a symbol of lifelong learning in cooking. Blue Apron encourages continuous learning by introducing members to new ingredients, flavors and cooking techniques with seasonally-inspired recipes that are always delicious, easy and fun to prepare.